"*The Truth About Work* abandons statistics and cold analysis in favor of an intuitive search for meaning in the world of work. David Harder's lecture style joins the growing body of work by motivational thinkers who also provide entrepreneurial insight."

—Vicki Torres
small business reporter, the *Los Angeles Times*

"Must reading for anyone who works or coaches those who do. David Harder prompts us to realize the truth about what is important in life and reminds us that our truth about work begins by the questions we ask ourselves . . . something only top coaches and mentors have known instinctively for centuries."

—Vance Caesar, Ph.D.
president/chair of the board,
The Professional Coaches and Mentors Association

"A new voice of courage, David Harder's truth is moving, potent, practical and profound. There is astonishing humor in *The Truth About Work*—that presentation prompted me to listen even more intently to the message."

—Emily Coleman
author, *Brief Encounters*

W9-BYB-366

The Truth About Work

Making a Life, Not a Living

David Harder

Health Communications, Inc.
Deerfield Beach, Florida

www.hci-online.com

Library of Congress Cataloging-in-Publication Data

Harder, David, date.
    The truth about work: making a life, not a living / David
Harder.
        p.   cm.
    Includes bibliographical references.
    ISBN 1-55874-465-7 (pbk. : alk. paper)
    1. Work—Psychological aspects.   2. Success—Psychological
aspects.   I. Title.
BF481.H36   1997   97-26300
158.7—dc21   CIP

©1997 David Harder

ISBN 1-55874-465-7

Publisher: Health Communications, Inc.
                   3201 S.W. 15th Street
                   Deerfield Beach, FL 33442-8190

Cover design by José Villavicencio

To Madeline Cummings,
"Mama Pumpkin."
Your spirit, wit, wisdom and,
above all, your love
inspired so many of us
to move beyond
ourselves.

Contents

Acknowledgments

A special thanks to Barbara J. Hodgson. Your insight and feedback led to a broader vision with *The Truth About Work*. Thank you for being such a strong and professional sounding board.

I also extend sincere thanks to . . .

Andrew Uris—your generosity made this possible. Wherever your heart is, you are a big player.

Bill Milham—my best friend, my instigator and touchstone. Thank you for inspiring me to take the leap seven years ago. Still jumping!

Jerry Ward—your loyalty and commitment inspired me to stick with it and stick with it, and oh, by the way, stick with it.

Debra Johnson—the easiest friend on earth to have. What a rock!

Sherry Geyer—for taking at least 3,000 stands with me. You are courage personified.

Bob Maurer—for being possibly the brightest person on earth.

Daniel Pollack—for teaching me how to have standards and to stand for a totally excellent adventure.

Kent Nethery—for being a brilliant and loving example of work as an act of love, and for your brotherhood.

Mike Greenberg—the most consistent healer I've ever met. It is a gift to have your friendship.

Emily Coleman—from leading nude encounter groups to signing up as Mom, you are enthusiasm and love personified.

Alice March—an elegant mind and soul. Thank you for the encouragement at the beginning of everything.

Sue Gould—being yourself inspired me to get bigger.

Jack Canfield—your instincts, love and generosity made this happen. You are the genuine article.

Amy Bonneau—for your courage, class and demonstration that we are on the right track.

Linda Schulze—for sitting in these seminars year after year—interested! You are gifted, and you are a gift!

Golda and Moyshe—you have kept me "off it" since you came into my life. Thanks for the sanity! You've earned more biscuits.

In *The Truth About Work,* you will be hearing from individuals who personify the themes I'm sharing with you in this book. My greatest privilege in writing *The Truth* was being able to meet with these powerful personalities to discuss their truth. For everyone who contributed, thank you from the bottom of my heart.

And finally, my thanks to my brilliant and loving business tribe: Chuck Balgenorth, Peter Cowen, Vance Caesar, Patricia Wisne, Ann Pilkington, Dennis Clark, Marcus Johns, Paul Liebeskind, Dana Menkus, Andrea Portenier, Linda Small, Gil Dawson, Diane Poliak, Dani Barr, Bambi Holzer and Suzanne Lopez.

Introduction

THE MACHINE HAS CONQUERED MAN,

[AND] MAN HAS BECOME A MACHINE,

WORKING BUT NO LONGER LIVING.

—MAHATMA GANDHI

Our old work world started collapsing in the late 1980s. For many of us, it seemed to happen overnight. In truth, our culture had been running toward it for a long time. The old world simply disappeared.

It happened to me. For years, I survived by manipulating the world of work as an executive in the search, placement and temporary help industries. Work was a necessary evil, an answer to a problem, and a challenge handed to me by parents, bosses, educators and advertising focus groups. It came in the form of a question: *How can I create enough income to ultimately escape the workplace?*

This wasn't an especially lofty standard, and yet it motivated and drove my entire relationship to work. I was getting ready for, driving to, being at, driving home from and recovering from something I wanted to leave. Passion and value, purpose and satisfaction, life work, meaning, joy, enchantment, spiritual fulfillment—all took a backseat to economic betterment.

A year before I had my own breakthrough, someone walked into my office and said, "You're so successful. How do you do it?" I responded, "In a coma." After moving thousands of people through the workplace, I had little evidence that spiritual and economic needs could be reconciled and sustained. The answer waited in a retirement plan or a lottery ticket.

From my vantage point in the employment industry, it was becoming clear that the old way of living, the very way of "being" in this thing we call "work," was fracturing and crumbling. And it was happening in virtually every profession and industry, from medicine to music, from banking to entrepreneurship. The few people I had encountered who were clearly passionate about their work had a healthy *relationship* with work, a relationship that contained much more than just making a successful choice.

I didn't just want a better choice. An entire career industry was focused on choice. I wanted my life purpose, and I wanted to succeed in that purpose. In other words, I wanted a life. My life. Not the life society was imposing on me, but the life God intended for me. Please understand that when I use the words *spiritual* and *God,* I'm coming not from a religious viewpoint, but rather, from the idea of having a fulfilled and healthy inner life. When I was a child, "God's will" had nothing to do with my personal happiness. As an adult, I've found that each one of us is given a unique potential, a unique purpose and a clear opportunity to live a fulfilling life. That purpose and opportunity are "God-given." The choices that lead to them are "life-giving." So many of us have been talked into believing, by our culture, that there are no choices. So we lose ourselves to our culture. But what our culture gives us has nothing to do with unique potential, unique purpose or a fulfilled life.

Some of us can see that. Some of us have reached the point where we know that, and yet, we don't know how to step over this last "hump." It is, perhaps, a most uncomfortable vantage point. Potential is a cruel thing when we can see it but don't yet know how to live in it.

Where are the tools? When I decided to move beyond the value and meaning of work that our culture imposed on me, I couldn't find those tools. I met career counselors who were miserable about their own careers, dispensing my "options." I enrolled in human-potential seminars with a built-in cultural pressure to "make a difference in the world." We were making declarations all the time: "Heal the rain forest," "Stop AIDS," "Build a new Los Angeles." All of this was good in the sense that I was making incremental progress. I certainly knew what I *didn't* want. Unfortunately, the necessary insight regarding my life purpose and how I could succeed in it eluded me. I've found that in our culture, many of us get stuck at this point. Quite simply, our culture gives us a great deal of evidence that we can't move beyond this point.

In the spiritual communities, I was having just as much trouble. Inner peace is fine, but where's the money? In fact, why is there so much contempt for making money?

A human-potential leader once told me, "In our culture, dysfunction is the norm." After working with thousands of people in intimate settings, I've come to the conclusion that it was an accurate assessment, but one that we need to change. Because in truth, "the norm" in how we approach, define and relate to work hasn't been very healthy, and is becoming progressively more uncomfortable to most of us.

In the old work world, "normal" work has been toil, monotony, politics, turf protection and a virtual "rodent wheel" of economic pursuit. Many of us have been falling off that wheel—some were laid off, some jumped off and some are just now becoming nauseous from going around one more time.

Getting off the wheel for good requires initiative. Most dictionaries define initiative as taking the first step, making the first move. That's true. Real initiative comes out of the awareness that you, quite simply, are enough. Once we recognize that each one of us is enough, we can give up the idea of helplessness in the face of a 200-year evolutionary "burp" called the industrial revolution.

The industrial revolution literally seduced the worker into trading a natural relationship to work with a time clock, monotony and artificiality. And for what? Predictability. Today, our nation grieves over the loss of predictability. We grieve over the loss of jobs replaced by a robot or software. And yet, many of us are not questioning the impact on the human spirit of a job so artificial it can be replaced with a machine and an electronic impulse.

The very nature of the human spirit is to change. Today, we find the human spirit prompting a "need to succeed" within virtually everyone we encounter in the workplace, a "need to succeed" in both the spiritual and economic worlds. If only our standards didn't get in the way!

When it comes to meeting the standards that have been used to define the meaning of work, most of us have the cards stacked against us. Finding our life purpose and getting paid well for living that purpose is as likely as winning the lottery because our standards for success are obsolete. For most of us, meeting the old standards of success means simply surviving, not thriving. Is forfeiting our life purpose and living a comatose existence good enough?

We will awaken from this comatose existence when we sincerely ask the questions: "Why am I here?" "What is the meaning I want to bring to my life?" Think about it. The only meaning we can *make* out of life is the meaning we *apply* to our lives. The moment we start asking these questions and exert the initiative to answer them, we stop looking the other way. How many of us have been looking the other way in our own lives, waiting for something to happen that hasn't happened and may never happen? And while this is occurring, life ticks on. The richness, the fulfillment and the awareness are for others—for those who've made a commitment to examine and use their own God-given birthright.

When we embrace initiative, when we recognize that we are enough, we can change our standards the way we can change our clothes. If the very nature and meaning of work are undergoing complete and revolutionary change, couldn't this be an opportunity to uplevel everything—i.e., to take a portion of our life or our entire life and raise our standards?

Our history works against this. Achieving both spiritual *and* economic fulfillment isn't the norm in our culture. I watched thousands of workers make employment changes when the boss from hell fired them, the company downsized, the market collapsed, the bills outgrew the salary or someone else got the promotion. Frankly, few people came in the doors of our employment agencies saying, "I want work that will serve my physical, spiritual, emotional and economic growth." But isn't it time we treat spiritual *and* economic fulfillment as the norm?

Most of us, to varying degrees, are living with "substandards," standards that actually work against the quality of our lives. These substandards come from a world that no longer exists. The requirements of working within industrial society are gone. That culture is dead. Yet it continues to exist in our words:

- "It's only a job."
- "No one likes what they do."
- "It's a living."

Using these substandards sucks the very life out of our work. In *The Truth About Work,* we're going to examine some of our stronger culturally held substandards. Here's one: I can only do my best work after driving through miles of hostile traffic, finding a subterranean parking space and sitting in a cubicle with fluorescent lights over-head.

The old work culture imposed the idea on many of us that if we get too comfortable, we can't do good work. For one moment, let's put on the sanity hat and ask the question: "Why?" Step back for just a moment and ask yourself: "Is this crazy?" Why do so many of us put up with a substandard experience of what we do with most of our waking hours, driven by the dream of a little high-quality leisure?

If each one of us has a unique, life-giving purpose, what is yours? Where is your place at the table? What are you here to do that no one else in this world is doing? Each and every one of us has utterly personal answers to these questions.

In the old world, we didn't ask questions like that. The old world embraced "either-or." We can *either* have a great career *or* a personal life. We can *either* make a great living for our family *or* be present for our family. We can *either* be happy with what we do for work *or* we can eat. We can *either* lead the company *or* be human. Why is it that so many people who are pursuing spiritually driven work are starving for money and that so many people striving for economic progress are spiritually starving? Why are some people still saying, "Don't pray for money"?

The end of every century has been marked by a revolution. Today, we are approaching the end of a millennium. It is marked by a redefinition of life as we know it and work as we know it—the final evolution beyond industry-based values. The change is challenging, ruthless, filled with opportunities and vicious for those who cling to the status quo. Our world has become ruthless to individuals and organizations that don't identify, promote and uphold the truth, for without truth, change just dumps us and leaves us behind. Witness IBM in the late 1980s, clinging to dependence on the mainframe computer as the world filled with PCs—perhaps the single greatest demonstration of organizational arrogance and its consequences. A few years later, IBM "snaps out of it," apparently embraces the truth and we see a dramatic turn in the company's fortunes.

The Truth About Work is designed to prompt you to question the meaning, nature and purpose of your life's work. It is designed to give you a structure to examine your own truth about work. The truth that is precious to you already exists. It doesn't need to be grandiose, and yet, it is grand. So, as we proceed, I encourage you to question everything—how you work, what you want. Question your organization. Question me. The human animal is not a guru. Gurus graduate from humanity and then get torn apart for acting as if they have the truth. If the truth already exists, I can't impart it to you. I can, however, coach, prod, irritate, entertain, comfort and even trick you into telling your truth.

We're human. Humans are fragile, vulnerable, imperfect and prone to making big mistakes. I am. For a moment, let's even try to play with the probability that all of us, in some way, are desperate. But what a spirit we have! If we use initiative, we can move beyond what our culture imposed on us and talked us into believing. In fact, if we use enough initiative, we can move beyond anger over buying the promises of the old work culture and finding that not only did we end up unfulfilled, but that the promises are no longer true.

As we move out of the old work culture, we're facing the last "hump." Some of us think it is as vast as the Grand Canyon and that we have to somehow jump over it—alone. Some of us view it, quite simply, as a speed bump—slow down a bit, make a quick assessment and move on. In truth, we can only manage this particular bump one person at a time. Most of us are ready to have full, rich, integrated lives in which we succeed in our work and in our home.

You can use *The Truth About Work* as a "casual read," one that gives you insights, a bit of entertainment. You can also use *The Truth About Work* with the initiative and commitment to use this information, apply it to your life and see how far you can take it. This will require more than a casual read. If that is what you want to do, take the time and energy to personalize each concept presented in this book to your own life. When you're done, if it doesn't work for you, don't use it.

If *The Truth* does what it is intended to do:

- You will question the very nature and meaning of your work.
- You will question the purpose you really have in the world.
- You will question how to use the revolution occurring around you for your benefit rather than your detriment.
- You'll have fun in the process.

Thousands of participants contributed to this information and these insights so that you could read this book in the comfort of your own home, on the beach, in the plane, on the treadmill—anywhere to help you stay off the rodent wheel.

If there is any single truth I can stand for, it is that each and every one of us has a unique life purpose and can live that purpose well. Inside of you, right now, is a spirit that wants you to plunge in. And inside of you, right now, are a series of beliefs that are begging you to run.

Your culture and your spirit are calling.

For Reflection

At the end of many chapters in The Truth About Work *there will be a few questions. I urge you to keep a notebook devoted to your truth about work and in it, write out each question, answering them as thoroughly and clearly as possible. By doing this, you will get much more value from* The Truth, *and it will personalize your outcome.*

1. What do you want to solve by reading and interacting with *The Truth About Work?*

2. What do you want to learn about yourself by reading this book?

3. What "substandards" do you have about work (standards that are the opposite of life giving)?

4. How do you view change in your workplace and in your life?

5. What is the breakthrough you want to have by the time you finish reading *The Truth About Work*?

The Revolution

GOD INTENDS NO MAN TO LIVE IN THIS WORLD
WITHOUT WORKING; BUT IT SEEMS TO ME NO
LESS EVIDENT THAT HE INTENDS EVERY MAN
TO BE HAPPY IN HIS WORK.

—JOHN RUSKIN

To begin, let's agree on one thing: The industrial revolution was killing us, and it's over. Some of us will immediately reject this idea with the statement that we never participated in the revolution. Some of us still think it was a good idea. For now, let's just engage in the concept. Throughout *The Truth About Work,* we're going to try on concepts. In the end, if you don't believe them or don't like them, *don't use them.* For now, just try using the ideas.

Regardless of the industry we work in or our professional title, whether we're high or low on the corporate ladder, student or dancer, entrepreneur or health-care worker, none of us totally escaped the tenets of the industrial revolution. These tenets were foisted on us as truth for over 200 years—artificial beliefs and behaviors imposed on us so deeply that at best, we've lost energy to them, and at worst, our authentic self has been drowned. During this time, many of us surrendered our adaptability and creativity through a seduction that began many years ago. Why did we willingly surrender ourselves to ideas and concepts that ran counter to our very biology? What will it take for us to stop suppressing our humanity? For over 200 years, we have adopted behavior in the workplace that works against our physical and emotional health. What happened?

Approximately 200 years ago, we came up with a new way to produce incomprehensible quantities of goods. We built factories: huge warehouses that had to be filled with cheap labor. We seduced workers to come in from the fields and ranches, to come out of the cobbler shops, all with the promise of predictability. Previously, workers' lives had been filled with a frightening unpredictability generated by weather, isolation and uncertain economics.

With the industrial revolution, we introduced the world of quantity. We standardized work by creating repetitive, simplified and rote routines. Workers fell into a daily, numbing ritual. We started overcoming our basic nature by treating ourselves as machines. Bolts in holes, sprockets in wheels, canisters, broomsticks and cars all poured forth while engineers created new, even more repetitive routines so that the system could take on even greater speed. The seduction, which in the 1970s and 1980s was referred to as "recruitment," centered on several unhealthy concepts. One was: "The company will take care of you." We became dependent on organizations for our well-being. In return, the company simply required us to become machine-like, to give up our humanity to production quotas.

Another unhealthy idea that emerged during this time was the idea that we do everything on our own. Independence was glamorized in the industrial culture. (We didn't point out that workers were totally dependent on the company.) We rewarded workers for what they did on their own and punished them if they gave each other too much attention or became too creative. In the world of quantity, there simply wasn't room for such needs.

Many of us bought into the promises of "the job." For centuries, we had managed just fine with *work,* but without *jobs*. Now we became enslaved by the very idea of the job, a contract with the captains of industry in which they gave us predictability and we gave them our humanity. Jobs were based on numbers, monotony, turf protection, known expectations, routine and the belief that all of this would continue until we got our gold watch. Our work and, ultimately, our lives were standardized. We clocked in, we clocked out.

Quite mistakenly, the concepts and routines were replicated in the service industries of the 1970s and 1980s. We continued to measure the value of the worker by how much standardized and monotonous work could be completed in a given period of time.

By now, we were living the "American dream": predictable money, in the land of the free. We felt powerful, our destinies protected by the biggest companies on earth: General Foods, General Motors, U.S. Steel, IBM, Texaco, Bank of America and Ford. We absorbed predictability to the point where we didn't have to think too much, didn't question too much. There was always television, a TV tray, frozen food, kids, a couple of cars in the garage, insurance if we got sick and a pension for when we grew old. Work, for many, was simply a necessary evil. I might hate pumping rivets, selling quotas, typing claims . . . but there's always a vacation in my future.

What happened when we removed predictability from this vacuous scenario? When we killed a president; when the media turned the floodlights on the underbelly of human behavior; when huge companies could no longer hold the purse; when baby boomers learned they would pay for Mom and Dad's pension without a meaningful one of their own; when Rush Limbaugh became a hero? What happened when information took on more value than machines and we replaced the world of quantity with the world of value?

The industrial revolution collapsed. Even the illusion that we were still in it disappeared. When that happened, a whole series of concepts we believed in vanished. Predictability, jobs for life, expectations defined for us, guarantees—gone! They were just concepts. The tricky part is that for 200 years, we treated these concepts as truth. As we shattered these illusions—as we lost a nation driven by leadership and vision, and removed predictability from work lives already malnourished—what did we get? I assert that the industrial revolution abandoned our culture with these characteristics built into virtually every worker: aimlessness, cynicism, contempt and resignation

We are in the midst of another revolution. As we enter the world of value, we find extraordinary opportunities to reconcile spiritual and economic needs. *Human* needs. How could we possibly see these opportunities through the filters of aimlessness, cynicism, contempt and resignation? In this new world, we ask questions that must be answered. Identifying our truth and the truth about our world is not only a critical part of our happiness and satisfaction; the truth is now critical to our survival.

Want to visit the ideal career development family? Here's how they respond to the new child:

> *Congratulations, kid! You've entered a world filled with risk and opportunity. We don't have a clue what your life purpose is. In fact, it would be arrogant for us to impose such assumptions on you. What we will give you is constant, high-quality attention and love. We'll do our best to help you get answers and to realize your unique value in the world. We'll do our best to impart good morals and character. We'll be permissive in your self-identity and celebrate as you define your unique gift, your individual purpose.*

How many of us grew up in families like that?

Most of us grew up in a world that taught us to be defined by people other than ourselves. Now we must answer these questions:

What is our life purpose?
Where is our greatest opportunity?
What's going to make us happy?

When we use cynicism, contempt, aimlessness and resignation, we can dismiss such questions. We don't even "try on" upleveling as a concept. This upleveling, a place beyond our old standards of survival, isn't even explored because we don't believe such a place exists.

Now, we are faced with a new world, the world of value. Everywhere we look, we see a loss of interest in numbers. People and organizations want value. We want the most for our dollar and our time.

The world of value requires real value from each and every one of us. As we transfer rote, monotonous and repetitive work to technology, each of us has to deliver real value. A dispassionate relationship with our work is no longer enough; we don't even get hired.

Work satisfaction? Life satisfaction? Many of us surrendered those to job descriptions, family expectations, professional titles—all in return for predictability. We didn't know better. As we return to questions of satisfaction and happiness, let's look at a basic truth: *Until we live our life purpose, we are not living our life. We are living someone else's life.* How can any of us be happy living someone else's life?

Recently, First Interstate Bank was dismembered by Wells Fargo Bank, another "megamerger." One of the executives called me and said the employees had lost their goodwill approximately 10 minutes after the merger announcement. He said they were angry, hostile and bitter. I responded that such feelings had little to do with Wells Fargo. Often, forced layoffs only beam a spotlight on our own aimlessness. The event illuminates our personal anger at walking through life without the awareness of why we are actually here. We rage at ourselves for buying into the illusion that if we surrender ourselves to a machinelike routine, we'll be "taken care of."

Almost all of us, when faced with or even reminded of our power, our potential, our very real capability of glory, have an immediate reaction. We run our potential for glory through these four filters:

- Aimlessness (I'm too busy to be extraordinary.)
- Cynicism (John Kennedy's assassination, the Nazis, Bangladesh—in a world like this, why go for "glory"?)
- Contempt (You've got no credentials to tell me this.)
- Resignation (Why bother? I'm stuck here.)

Our culture has trained us to dismiss our own power. Our culture no longer has "the truth." The truth exists inside of you. Truth is needed to succeed within this new world. Here's the revolution. Our truth existed in the old world as well, but in this new world, we need to act on the truth in order to survive. Corporate mission statements won't do it. Personality tests won't define it. Only your personalized truth matters here. Getting to that truth requires walking past our filters. It fundamentally means shifting from a core response of "no" to "yes." Yes, let's do it. Yes, let's try it. Yes, this is my truth.

Why is this turning point so critical? In the world of real value, everything changes. In this new world, a mediocre relationship with one's work doesn't produce enough value or generate enough energy to even survive. In this new world, clocking in and clocking out isn't enough. The technology is in place to free people from performing all tasks that are dull and monotonous. That may be scary, and yet, there is an enormous opportunity here for us to identify our personal truth in our work. In front of us is the opportunity to live our lives and do our work as individuals. The assembly lines are going, the jobs are going and the standardized life is going as well. Oscar Wilde said:

> *Selfishness is not living as one wishes to live. And unselfishness is letting other people's lives alone, not interfering with them. Selfishness always aims at creating around it an absolute uniformity of type. Unselfishness recognizes infinite variety of type as a delightful thing, accepts it, acquiesces in it, enjoys it.*[1]

Infinite variety of type. Welcome to the new work world! No standardized lives. Discarding our filters prompts us to wake up. Is that uncomfortable? I personally wasn't joyous when I realized I had been partially asleep for a good portion of my adult life. Dysfunction didn't teach me to uplevel my life. The avenue out came from paying attention to the people who had upleveled their lives successfully. Studying individuals who had defined their life purpose and were succeeding in their life purpose gave me the insights. The great behavioral scientist Robert Maurer says, "Nothing of value happens in this world without collaboration." To succeed in this new world, we must find the collaborators who can show us the way.

How do we make it in this revolutionary world? How do we uplevel our standards? First, we choose to. This choice

---

1. Dale Carnegie, *Dale Carnegie's Scrapbook* (New York: Simon & Schuster, 1959), 186.

requires the destruction of our cynicism, aimlessness and contempt. The act of choosing automatically takes us out of resignation. The moment we choose to get rid of the norm, all our beliefs, behaviors and ideas become suspect.

There are only three basic choices in life. We can live fully, heal fully or do something else. Living fully simply means we are out there doing what we want to do, taking risks, being creative and adaptive. We're involved with our lives. Oh, periodically, we crash and burn. For those of us who have committed to full living, though, we get back up and participate.

For those of us who want to live fully but can't, we need to heal fully. Carl Jung said, "Before we can see the light, we have to walk in the shadow." Unfortunately, in our culture, this is a very unpopular process. Healing isn't serene! It's uncomfortable. Full healing takes earnest and steadfast commitment. Full healing requires healers who actually heal us rather than treating us as wounded forever. Healing often requires discomfort.

In our culture, the norm in the face of discomfort is distraction. How many of us have practiced creative thinking while watching television, eating good food, in-line skating? On average, we work 40 years, during which time most of us sleep about 13 years. We watch television an average of six and a half years. Why bother with healing? Why bother with getting to our lives? We're too distracted! While we're distracted, we're thinking about getting creative, we're thinking about changing our lives, we're thinking about the problem.

Creative thinking is not creativity. Creativity is a risk- and action-filled event. We cannot remove risk from action. Creative thinking does not include risk or action. Silvano Arieti said, "The world's mental institutions are filled with creative thinkers." Many of us have been conditioned to avoid risks at all costs. So as we come out of a world filled with predictability, television and creative thinking, we often settle for a third life choice: snivelin'.

Snivelin' protects our aimlessness. It is based on the belief that we are helpless and buys into the belief that someone owes us. Snivelin' justifies our not living up to our true purpose because there is no true purpose.

Living, healing, snivelin': If we choose to "snap out of it," we find a startling new awareness of work and of life. We find ourselves in a world filled with purpose and value. In front of us is a new revolution that demands our full participation and requires each one of us to identify, uphold and promote our truth. *Our truth.* Today, we are faced with a rate of change that demands constant exploration and definition regarding the truth about our world and our role in the world.

Living, healing or snivelin': If we fully participate in this new revolution, what's the payoff? Could it be a world where our work reflects personal values? Could we be entering a world where purpose and our awareness of purpose are the norm? I assert that this is where we are headed. I assert that the train has already left the station. If you haven't come on board, run! What is left behind will be dreadful.

In this new world of value, our consciousness is the key to succeeding. The world of quantity is already decaying, and the workers clinging to that corpse are giving a new meaning to the term *have nots*. In the world of real value, we must define our purpose. As we do so, each one of us experiences a value we could never have in the world of quantity. This is a revolution!

Remember the 1980s? In Los Angeles, we were selling $3 million homes made out of cardboard and built on top of landfills. Today, we are no longer casual about how we spend our money. We are looking for value. In this world, we have to define our own value in the workplace. Only a definition of authentic value works. Everything else is, quite simply, irrelevant.

What I'm proposing here isn't necessarily easy. Our old world has been killed off. Stepping out of that world requires killing off what's old, comfortable, obsolete, perhaps even ugly, within ourselves. Letting go of our old definition of self means killing off the old self. This has to occur for the new, authentic self to emerge. A valuable destruction? Absolutely! Easy? Usually not.

It isn't done alone. It requires support, coaching and mentors. A high-quality transition requires high-quality support and sound information—on a daily basis. I have worked with thousands of clients and seminar participants, from all walks of life, as they opened themselves up and produced the miracle of jumping from the old world to the new world. After watching so many people successfully do this, I've reached the conclusion that our core fear in changing ourselves centers around fear of dying. We are killing off the person we've known for so long. Killing off the sniveler, the person who has bought into other people's expectations, the person who is willing to have partial work health but is not willing to pay the price for a holistic experience.

What is in this new revolution that could be interesting

and valuable for us? Remember the brief history of the old work revolution. Let's revisit the American workplace:

Xerox, a former recruiter of corporate ladder-climbers, eliminates 16,000 management positions. The organization collapses into a flat structure, axing the old paternalistic "job-for-life" employment contract and replacing it with the "employability" contract. Under this new contract, there is no ladder to climb and very little rote or monotonous work. The worker has to demonstrate value. The work is stimulating and interesting. In doing the work, you become "more employable," more valuable in the market, and the responsibility for defining and marketing that value is yours.

A librarian becomes disillusioned with an antiquated bureaucracy, an organization too cumbersome to keep up with the times. She becomes weary of an environment that doesn't give her the kind of value and recognition she wants. This soft-spoken librarian develops a new library on the Internet. Two years later, she is running the largest library in the world and making over $300,000 per year.

Manpower, a temporary-help service, becomes the nation's largest private employer.

A CEO runs his multinational business from a 75-foot sailboat. An investment consultant researches, develops, sells and transmits his national stock-advisement service from a home in Sedona. A copywriter moves out of an office building and does her work on the beach, her Powerbook transmitting data back to her employer. Professional baby boomers flood Coeur d'Alene in Idaho and Telluride in Colorado, telecommuting so they can have more flexible time and raise their families in healthier environments.

A highly competitive sales organization hires sales professionals with young children. The employees "job share," which allows them to spend more time with their children. The company also benefits by getting two minds and two client bases for the price of one person.

Workers, fed up with all the consequences of being treated as overhead, outsource their own jobs, turning their work into businesses. A human resources executive outsources her entire operation, selling the services back to the company as a profit-making enterprise.

A defense industry laser engineer, tired of building nuclear warheads, gets laid off. When he commits to upleveling his entire life, he finds a job with Disney Imagineering, where he helps design amusement rides.

Poor, lost "Generation X" produces more new millionaires than any other portion of our culture and any previous generation.

We move from "job orientation" to "work consciousness." This means we can now evaluate options suited to our lifestyle. A few of the packaging choices include independent contractor, job holder, telecommuter, job sharer, temporary, freelancer, small-business owner, project worker, outsourcer.

In the new revolution, fortunes are being made, old industries disappearing, new opportunities springing up everywhere. In the new revolution, the filters of aimlessness, cynicism, contempt and resignation must be replaced with purpose, true creativity, adaptability and, above all, something to get passionate about! Jane Applegate, the author of *Succeeding in Small Business,* identified several fatal mistakes for small-business owners. She told me, "The most fatal of all small-business mistakes is to do something you don't love." If we don't love it, we fail to generate the passion and energy necessary to succeed in the world of value. In this new world, we need these components regardless of the way we package our work.

In *The Truth About Work,* we're going to talk about exploiting change. How do we use it to better our lives rather than to our detriment? There are two differing vantage points we can work from:

- Change is detrimental, and I'm going to use this book to "cope better." (Passivity)
- Change is constant, and I'm going to use it to my benefit. (Initiative)

What would it take for you to be spiritually and economically satisfied? What kind of workplace generates optimum well-being without having to check our spirit at the door? In the chapters that follow, we're going to have conversations with some of the individuals who are succeeding in the spiritual and economic worlds. What are they doing that's different from what the rest of us are doing? If we are going to realize our unique purpose in the world, what has to change in us? If we are going to give up cynicism, contempt, aimlessness and resignation, what will we have to change first?

For many of us, we have to start with reevaluating the erroneous, unhealthy and ugly information we've been given about fear. Fear was built into our biology. For those of us who don't get past first base, it is usually because we have been given total untruth about the world of fear.

For Reflection

1. If you thoroughly exploited change to serve your economic and spiritual fulfillment, what would the outcome look like?

2. Within the context of real value, how would you define your purpose?

3. What steps would you be comfortable taking right now to begin to get past the four filters (aimlessness, cynicism, contempt, resignation)?

4. What is the greatest risk you would have to assume in order to do what you really want to?

5. What are the indications that you have been living someone else's life, rather than your own?

World of Quantity	World of Value
Numbers	Value
Survival	Satisfaction
Goods and Services	Intelligence
Job Description	Life Purpose
Compartmentalized Lives	Integrated Lives
Predictability	Chaos
Emotionally Suppressed	Emotionally Permissive
Organizational Hierarchy	Flat Organization
Covert	Truth-Based
Quota Foundation	Spiritual Foundation

2

The Truth About Fear

OFTEN WHEN THE HEART IS TORN WITH SORROW,
SPIRITUALLY WE WANDER LIKE A TRAVELER LOST IN A
DEEP WOOD. WE GROW FRIGHTENED, LOSE ALL SENSE
OF DIRECTION, BATTER OURSELVES AGAINST TREES AND
ROCKS IN OUR ATTEMPT TO FIND A PATH. ALL THE WHILE
THERE IS A PATH—THE PATH OF FAITH—THAT LEADS
STRAIGHT OUT OF THE DENSE TANGLE OF OUR
DIFFICULTIES INTO THE OPEN ROAD WE ARE SEEKING.

—HELEN KELLER

G od didn't create fear as a feeling to oppress us, but
as a mechanism to take us into action. That's all.
What prompted us to use fear as a tool for oppression? As a culture, what did we have to gain by
creating all these untruths about fear?

We respond to fear by taking action or getting paralyzed. What we do with it has nothing to do with "separating the men from the boys." Nothing. That is another untruth. Some of the men reading this book are already saying, "I'm not frightened!" Remember, testosterone doesn't overcome fear. It's for fighting and sex. Some women have taken on the belief that they have to act as if testosterone were coursing through their veins in order to succeed, albeit at great cost. "Don't be frightened" is the basic oppositional untruth coursing through our culture.

The only purpose of fear is to take us into action. Therefore, fear is just fine. Fear isn't a feeling that was meant to overcome and paralyze us. Fear is actually a mechanism in our nervous system, designed to prompt action. Our culture made up stories and interpretations about fear, either to dominate others or to avoid the feeling altogether. The words bandied around about fear usually boil down to "Don't be frightened" or "There's something wrong with being frightened." All the while, it is a mechanism designed into each of our bodies that takes us into action. It is our words and interpretations that get in the way of that action.

Nelson Mandela's nervous system is designed basically the same way as Bo Derek's. Dr. Ruth has a fear mechanism built into her nervous system that follows the same basic design as Boris Yeltsin's. All of these people have widely different beliefs, stories and interpretations of fear, given to them by their culture. Our fear mechanism is given to us by our biology.

Early on, kings, warlords, captains of industry, parents, churches and, yes, even the rest of us recognized that we could use these stories about fear to dominate, manipulate and control others. Domination occurs in the midst of ignorance about a particular issue. It's easy to be dominated and controlled if we are conditioned into believing there is anything wrong with fear.

My dogs see a cat, and they chase the cat. When the cat snarls and swipes back, the female dog turns warrior and the male dog howls and runs to me. They're not caught up in the words of our culture; they're taking action. Fight or flight isn't about "Should I be afraid or not afraid?" It's about "What action should I take as a response to my alarm going off?"

How about taking a look at a few untruths and truths about fear? First the untruths:

- "This seminar will give you the tools to get rid of fear forever!"
  (Don't be frightened.)
- "Even though Engulf and Devour Corporation has just purchased your company, we are not planning any staff changes."
  (Don't be frightened.)
- "Shut up, or I'll really give you something to be frightened about."
  (Don't be frightened.)
- "Paralyzed by fear? Take Prozac."
  (Don't be frightened.)

Now let's take the same untruths and add the subtext of truth:

- "This seminar will give you the tools to get rid of fear forever!"

(No seminar does that. At best, a program will educate you on what fear really is.)

- "Even though Engulf and Devour Corporation has just purchased your company, we are not planning any staff changes."
  (Dust off your résumé. This company has fired over 50,000 employees after making statements like this. It is a ruse designed to buy time. If you end up being a "survivor," be sure to leave forwarding numbers for your friends and family. You'll work 60-hour weeks but, if you're really lucky, you'll receive a free turkey on Thanksgiving.)

- "Shut up, or I'll really give you something to be frightened about."
  (Partially true. Full truth: You are being attacked by a slothful parent or adult. This individual doesn't understand fear, and someone who doesn't understand fear is quite frightening. If this person is a parent, he or she has taken on the most demanding job on earth. This individual is trying to turn it into a part-time job.)

- "Paralyzed by fear? Take Prozac."
  (You have created an illusion, both for yourself and for others, that you are no longer frightened. Unfortunately, now you can't access enough of your fear to take complete action in your life. It's a bit like a sailboat in a calm: floating, not really moving. The drug can be valuable in a crisis. But it is not a substitute for full living because we cannot live fully if we don't get frightened.)

When introducing the topic of fear, I'm commonly interrupted with, "Oh, you're talking about fight or flight." Right! If we step out into the street this afternoon and a big truck comes roaring around the corner, are we going to stand there and debate whether to fight or flee? *Let's see, should I stand up to this 7,000-pound machine hurtling toward me or run for my life?* Action is instantly called up by our nervous system; philosophical interpretation only gets in the way. The fear mechanism instantly pours some of the most potent chemicals and hormones known to humankind into our body, prompting us to run for our lives. Without this mechanism, we would be dead.

For centuries, our political, industrial and religious cultures gave us variations on "Don't be frightened":

- "Don't be frightened—we've got work to do."
- "Don't be frightened—God will take care of you."
- "Don't be frightened—I'm in charge."

Oh, there is a possibility of a world without fear—and yet, we're in a world with plenty to get frightened about. Metal detectors are in the doorways of our schools. We can get our tires shot out while driving to work. The big company we thought was going to employ us forever merges out of existence in a few months. Markets change. Jobs move "offshore." Managed care dries up income sources and creates new ones. We didn't think it would turn out like this.

For 20 years, I've encountered thousands of individuals doing rote, monotonous work they don't care about. They punch in, and they punch out. The less we care, the less we fear. We select whatever provokes the least passion, the least emotion, only to find fear flooding into our systems when the picture changes.

Life purpose? Passion? Meaning? Nah! In our old work culture, the idea was foisted on us that stepping out of our culture exacted too big a price. It was easier and safer to seek refuge in a job for life or in a profession. With the industrial machine, we got standardized lives, security and a routine. Life was often done for us, on our behalf. Spiritual and economic evolution have destroyed that model and removed the illusion that we're safe settling for the old way of living. Real safety occurs through our connection with spirit. Many of us don't know how to get there. We're too busy running on the "rodent wheel," hoping that compulsive movement will change something. Unfortunately, we don't even slow down to ask the question "What does my spirit want?" Some of us are frightened there won't be an answer, and some of us are frightened there will.

There's an old Chinese proverb: "He who asks a question is a fool for five minutes; he who does not ask a question remains a fool forever." Isn't it time that we question everything we believe about fear?

Spiritual and economic evolution present us with a crossroads: Step into our God-given life purpose and have a life or cling to the old work models and be swept away. Frightening? This represents a whole new world of "haves" and "have-nots."

From several vantage points, we get the appearance of no solution, of "five minutes of being a fool." At the very core, our aberrant reactions to fear paralyze us and we miss the opportunity that is in front of us: the opportunity that emerges by questioning everything about our life. Getting to this opportunity means having to dig through layers of beliefs until we reach our truth. For some of us, waking up to the realization that our lives have been molded and shaped around avoiding fear—and realizing that we are still frightened—becomes either a joke, bad news, a strange dream or a nightmare.

How many of us have lives shaped by the avoidance of fear? And how many of us, in truth, still get frightened? In fact, some of us are far more frightened than ever because business and spiritual evolution keep clawing away at us and we've avoided taking action for far too long.

The generations before us fought two world wars, lived through the Great Depression, one plague after another. It was tough! Baby boomers, on the other hand, were taught to avoid discomfort. It was our birthright. Our parents were frightened for us and wanted to shield us from a "sad" truth: Life can be tough!

A full life is filled with risks, challenges, victories and disasters, which many of us were taught to avoid. In doing so, many of us were not aware of the fact that this "fright thing" has become so big we can't even voice it. How many of us built lives of mediocrity around the illusion that we could avoid fear? And what was the price we paid?

A premise from the industrial revolution was that if we fit into its work culture, we would be shielded from fear. If we filled the quotas, life would be done for us. Usually, working in such a place required making a contract that culturalized shame if we felt any fright at all. Why should we be frightened if life is being done for us? We would get recruited from college by a Fortune 500 company, work 30 years, climbing the corporate ladder, marry, have two children, retire and die. Who told us everything would change? Who told us few recruiters would show up? That we'd have to turn into these mobile workers, moving from project to project or hiding behind our doors, hoping the human resources "death angel" wouldn't show up? We had so many illusions that kept us immobilized while all God wanted to do was make sure we would avoid the truck.

God and evolution built a mechanism into each of us that prompts us to take action, to succeed, and that saves our lives and creates possibilities by taking us into action. All of this happens if we simply allow the mechanism to work—when we give up the insane illusion of "risk aversion."

What are the mechanics of fear, and how do we humanize our entire relationship to fear?

Several years ago, Dr. Robert Maurer was a teaching psychologist at UCLA Medical School. He had just finished reading a book called *Plagues and Peoples*. Each plague ended not by studying the sick people, but by studying the people who were healthy and determining what was different about them. Dr. Maurer reasoned that if you followed this line of thought, then most therapeutic practices couldn't be that effective because they were based on the study of sick people. What would happen, he wondered, if we studied people who were succeeding in every area of their lives and found out what they were doing differently from the rest of us?

For the next several years, Dr. Maurer and his team collected studies of people who fit his definition of success. They were: "loving, lovable, stress resistant; happy about their work, happy about their family lives, happy about their finances, happy about their romantic lives, happy about their physical and emotional health."[1]

What did these astonishing people do with fear? Did they wrestle with it, overcome it, ignore it, succumb to it? There is a two-part answer. First: "Successful people are used to the experience of fear."[2] In other words, successful people don't steer around fear, don't treat fear as a bad thing when it shows up and don't act as if there were something wrong with encountering it. For them, fear isn't a big deal.

It is our interpretations of fear that produce stress. The cultural beliefs we carry around about fear are the primary cause of stress. Who taught us fear is "unnatural"? Our culture did.

Humans adapt by interpreting information and taking appropriate action. The information doesn't have to be true. When we embrace all of these cultural interpretations, when we embrace untruths, we are training our cerebral cortex, that human-unique brain department, to override what the body and the nervous system want and need. Our body may want skinless chicken and steamed vegetables. Our culture has taught us that Häagen-Dazs is more satisfying. Our culture taught us there is something wrong with fear, and our culture is nuts!

1. As heard in Dr. Maurer's seminar, "How Successful People Succeed." This program was delivered at UCLA Extension and UCLA Medical Center, Santa Monica. It has also been delivered in Careermotion's seminar, "The Discovery Program."
2. Maurer.

My colleagues and I have been using Robert Maurer's information regarding fear for six years. Today, having our fear mechanisms go off is treated with the same level of significance as going to the bathroom. It is needed, natural and periodically urgent. It is, in fact, biological. It is, however, no big deal.

"Used to the experience of fear." Pay attention to the most successful people in the world. Listen to them. Hear Olympic gold medalist Kerry Strug talk about how frightened she was when it was time to perform with her injury. When *Los Angeles Magazine* interviewed TV sitcom star Ellen DeGeneres about her rise from obscure comedy clubs to international stardom, she was asked how she felt about her success. She responded, "This raises my terror to a whole new level."[3]

Success isn't stopped by fear. It is supported by a natural *relationship* to fear, one that recognizes the needs of the mechanism. This brings us to Robert Maurer's second finding about success behavior and fear: "When frightened, successful people reach out for comfort."[4]

Our alarm mechanism requires comfort from other humans in order to shut down after it goes off. Otherwise, it continues to produce the hormones and chemicals designed to take us into action. Look at it as a spigot. To turn off a spigot, we turn the handle. In our nervous system, to shut off the alarm, we get comforted by another human. It's that simple. However, when successful

---

3. R. Daniel Foster, "Cover Q & A: New Girl," *Los Angeles Magazine*, v. 39, no. 10, Nov. 1994: 32-34.
4. Maurer.

people are frightened, they reach out for comfort and then move on.

Did you ever notice that kids do the same thing? When frightened, most children run to us, crying. We pick them up and comfort them. Their fear mechanism stops. We set them down. They move on. In fact, most of them simply go on as if nothing happened. When we repress this need as an adult, fright becomes a dysfunctional event. What could have prompted us to stop providing something so basic to our biological needs? When we take on erroneous information about fear, our bodies train us to avoid fear.

The mechanics of fear have been "hardwired" into our nervous system. Whenever that alarm goes off, the powerful chemicals pour out and we are ready to take action. Getting comforted is the event our alarm system requires, like food, in order to shut down. Without that event, it simply keeps running. Can you imagine what happens to a body that continues to get these chemicals? We get paralyzed, sick, "stressed out." We quickly and erroneously learn it is best to avoid triggering the mechanism.

What would it look like if we were *okay* with fear and naturally reached out for comfort? There would be a much higher probability we would tell the truth about our work. Without a healthy reaction to fear, truth has no place to reside. So, we often avoid the truth:

- "Yep, they've laid off another 3,000 employees, but they're not going to get me."
  (Nothing's certain; we can only increase the probability of success by taking action.)

- "I love my job."
  (I believe that all work sucks. So even though I work 700 hours a month with inadequate support, it's better than most jobs.)
- "I've launched an aggressive sales campaign."
  (I'm terrified of selling, so I've deluded myself into thinking that two sales calls per week is aggressive.)

If every time we got frightened, we said to ourselves, "It's *okay* to be afraid" and went to someone for comfort, if we expressed our fear, got our mechanism shut down and moved on, would life be more satisfying? Of course! We would progress to a more natural and humane way of living.

But before we go there, let's agree on one concept: In this culture, dysfunction is the norm. We seek comfort in dysfunctional ways. When frightened, we: drink alcohol, smoke cigarettes, become abusive, shut down, eat a layer cake, throw up, become "political," give up, destroy people, hide out, wait and see what happens, lie, become mean spirited, become aloof, become overpowering, become victims, confront inappropriate people, become hopeless, become overly optimistic, blame others, blame our parents, watch Jerry Springer, shop, work out too much, spread gossip, watch too much television, blame the company, sexually harass a subordinate, act impervious.

So where do we get comfort? Assuming we recognize that fear is a healthy emotion and a basic component in taking risks, growing and succeeding, there are only two forms of getting healthy comfort:

1. Reaching out to someone
2. Reaching out for education

What happens when we establish work cultures in which risk is expected and getting comforted is encouraged? As business markets flood with change, isn't it crucial to establish work environments where voicing fear is encouraged and we are actually rewarded for bringing it up? Rewarded with comfort, encouragement, even inspiration? Wouldn't we perform more effectively if it were natural and *okay* to say, "I don't know how to do this. Who can help?"

In a culture of mediocrity, we never get close enough to the action to actually become frightened. When frightened, however slightly, we reach for distraction: buy a video game, jump on the Internet, turn on the television, "wait for our ship to come in." We observe the possibilities, but actually jumping seems "too frightening." We run from the possibilities, too frightened to explore the potency God has designed into this gift, this thing called life.

Anaïs Nin said, "Life shrinks or expands according to one's courage." Today, we need your courage, your full living—not just a piece of your living. Quite frankly, our world of value can't fully live without your courage. If there is any doubt about that, look for a moment, with truth, at the world around you. As we remove jobs, assembly lines, middle managers and rote/repetitive work from our culture, anyone directly impacted by that is faced with a complete redefinition of life as we know it. Historically, "have-nots" were picked up by our welfare systems. As these systems disappear, what is to become of them? If we don't respond, what is to become of us?

I'm frightened for the have-nots because I can't see how they will survive in this new world. The spiritual, evolutionary and economic bars are being raised. If we don't educate them, I see a scenario for a war that will make political and national wars pale in comparison. At the core, war is about economics and the belief that there isn't enough for everybody. If we create two classes, people who know how to create value and people who don't even know how to survive, we have an economic scenario that is all too frightening. We urgently need to take action, to educate ourselves, our children, our communities. The emerging world of value apparently has no room for have-nots.

Some of us are not even engaging in this conversation because we're "too frightened." Many of us have been building our spirituality in a monastic way, going inward, praying and meditating. Evolution has raised the bar on us, and it is now time to answer these questions. Because now, we must take that spirit into the community. If every time we get frightened, we fall into prayer and meditation rather than taking action with the people who need our action, we have created a new form of dogma: the dogma of spiritual escapism.

I am not dismissing the value of and need for a solid spiritual foundation. That foundation requires introspection and connectedness with our inner life. But spiritual evolution is pressing us to move outward and contribute what we have; because once we realize we have a soul, we realize the have-nots are part of the same spirit. In truth, we are that connected.

Let's take a stroll through that world of have-nots. In the new work world, we find have-nots hiding in their offices, hoping the human resources "death angel" won't find them until retirement. For years, these workers have been rewarded for what they did on their own. It's "too frightening" to change. Funny, they often are the last ones to admit they're scared. Usually, we hear about the company abandoning them. It's someone's fault. At the core is a belief that waking up is simply too painful. They need our courage.

The new have-nots don't adopt the new work behavior. Reach out? Reveal skill deficits? Tell anyone that, "In truth, I don't have a clue"? In the old work world, we couldn't say that. In the new one, for most of us, most of the time, this is the truth: We need help. We don't have a clue. The new, more humane world of work requires that we work together on solutions. Nothing happens in a vacuum. In the old work culture, if we spoke our truth, we were commonly shown the door. Everyone shook their heads about poor Joe "losing it." How lost we were. The industrial culture suppressed our fear and dismissed our truth because it was all secondary to "getting the job done."

In the new world, have-nots wall themselves off from answers by acting as if they have the answers. They need our courage and comfort.

The quality of our comfort is equally important to success. In coffeehouses, we find starving artists, hanging out with other starving have-not artists, ranting and raving about the "burden of being gifted and misunderstood." They provide agreement to each other—sympathy, it's called. "It is so tough to be an artist." But sympathy is not comfort. Sympathy is the agreement to failure or grief. It is valid with grief. When it's used to give agreement to your troubles, run! We change by working with someone who is succeeding in the area in which we want to succeed. A mentor or a coach won't give us sympathy. They'll give us comfort, inspiration and education.

People who are healthy about fear hold the child until the crying stops. Then they send the child back into the game and, if the need arises, show the child how to play the game. If the child wants to play a different game, the comforter will often say, "It's okay to make mistakes. Everyone makes mistakes." As adults, we never biologically outgrow the need to be held and sent back into the game.

Business owners aren't immune to unhealthy beliefs regarding fear: Be strong, be independent, don't cry and, above all, compete, compete, compete. At worst, they go out of business. At best, they become enslaved by their work. Healthy and successful business owners are the most dependent creatures I know.

Listen! There are no secrets to success. The information is out in the open. It is our listening, or perhaps our lack of listening, that blocks reality and creates "secrets." Funny how we are never in on the secret. We use a language that lets us off the hook and allows us to slip back into the safety of aimlessness, contempt, cynicism and resignation. A successful life—do we measure it by the quantity of days or the quality of life? If we center our attention on getting through life without fear, without being hurt, without any harm, what have we added to the world? What have we generated in our own world?

The industrial revolution supported fear paralysis, conditioned us to work in independence, trained us to pursue life without risk and punished us if we voiced our fears. In other words, we embraced untruth about the mechanics of fear and the mechanics of being human. We were asked to mimic machines. In this new world of value, that's deadly stuff.

Survivors of organizational restructurings are often in greater distress than the people who were laid off. In the old work culture, support systems grew primarily in an environment of covertness. The industrial work culture pitted workers against each other, in competition for another "step up the ladder." Layers of bureaucracy shielded workers from each other. There wasn't a big need for truth because it was defined for us.

Our support systems took years to develop. In *The Truth About Work,* the support systems we use when frightened are called "comfort tribes." A comfort tribe is a group of people actively dedicated to our well-being. Perhaps you can now see that we are an animal that needs attention, comfort and other humans in order to succeed. Without each other, we don't take action; we are paralyzed with fear and too "stressed-out" to move on.

Layoffs and restructurings quickly destroyed these marginal comfort and support systems. Paralysis ensued. Today, flat work structures force people to collaborate, tell the truth and work as a team. To do that effectively, workers usually need intervention and training. Teams in the world of value bear little resemblance to the teams of the 1980s. Usually, the term "team player" just meant we had to work harder. It had nothing to do with being comforting, encouraging, risk oriented, fright permissive, truth centered and collaborative.

For the last 200 years, we've suppressed any display of fear, particularly in the workplace. Artificial behaviors have been imposed on us to suppress anything outside of being machinelike: on time, dependent, not in need of much attention, quiet and quantity driven. In doing this, we built a culture of mediocrity. The norm in our culture is to have a mediocre relationship with work, to settle for survival. In avoiding fear, we become dependent on distraction, dependent on vacations, just to get through another day.

Monkeys do better jobs with these fear basics than many of us. When threatened with danger, when fright-ened, regardless of whether they are in the jungle or in a controlled setting, what do the monkeys do first, before anything else? They run toward each other, and touch, grab and hug each other.

It has been said that the truth will set us free, but first it will make us angry. From my point of view, the truth saves us, and it can terrify us. Most of us need to be com-forted as we encounter the truth. Today, in truth, many of us crave a highly-principled work environment: a workplace filled with creativity, high-quality attention, dignity, truth telling, innovation, fun. We are starting to realize that environments filled with these qualities are actually far more productive than environments that try to engender productivity with just a corporate mission statement and a time clock. Excellence, in any culture, is generated by ongoing inspiration.

How do we get to ongoing inspiration? First, we rebuild

our personal viewpoint and response to fear so that whenever it shows up, we recognize that a biological mechanism is at work. We take the necessary action, and that action becomes a collaborative effort. It means that when we get frightened, we recognize there is nothing wrong with us and something has to happen. In this new culture, we recognize that isolation and creative thinking, linked together, are deadly to life purpose. We humanize ourselves by reaching out for comfort from another human, not a thing, not a distraction, not a behavior.

Next, in changing our awareness from having fear own us to recognizing that a system we own is at work, we move to building a comfort tribe. The tribe is made up of people committed to our well-being. Some of us, when we start looking at this issue, become aware that certain people who don't support our taking risks and don't comfort us when we get frightened may be currently in our circle. Often, we have individuals who still use shame as a tool to oppress the way we are. That is another norm. There is nothing new, nothing creative here. They are simply doing what has been done in our culture for centuries. Linking fear, shame and oppression has been going on for hundreds of years. It's called protecting ourselves by dominating others. Nothing new here. We ask for help, and they tell us we shouldn't need it. We tell someone we are frightened, and they give us reasons why we shouldn't be frightened.

What would happen if, as a culture, we became totally permissive about fear? First, we'd get rid of the word *should*. For a few minutes, let's replace the word *should* with *okay*. It's okay to . . .

be afraid
have a job
be happy
not be happy
ask for attention
be human
be confused
need comfort
have skill deficits
need collaborators
need coaches
make mistakes
make a mess
leave
get assistance
draw attention to ourselves
fail
lose
make millions

Comfort tribes recognize we are where we are. There's nothing wrong with the spot we're in unless *we* say there is something wrong. Comfort tribes give us comfort freely. Members of such tribes are generous, and they are generous in asking for help when they need it.

How do we overcome centuries of dysfunction and untruth and misuse of fear? We start with one pure word: generosity. We've lived in a world not particularly generous about having fear. A revolution? How about getting really generous with each other about fear?

Today, as risk shows up in our lives, as our colleagues

and intimate friends pursue their vision and commitments, fear shows up all the time. What would happen if we responded generously with ourselves and with each other? If we discussed it, came up with solutions to problems, comforted each other, watched out for each other? No one would beat the other up for encountering something that is normal for anyone who is living fully. Full living! Isn't even the prospect of full living prompting us to have this dialogue? Living fully and taking risks produce vulnerability. What if we gave our friends and colleagues the comfort they need to be vulnerable with risks? Gave them generosity and comfort? What do you think would happen to the quality of communication? To profitability?

Vulnerability is a quality that wasn't encouraged in the old industrial work culture. Oddly enough, it is a requirement for success in the new work culture, regardless of whether we are working in a big company or small company, or are self-employed. Whatever the work packaging, vulnerability simply means we could get "wounded or injured." We're "open." This is one of the reasons women are having a bit more ease with fitting into flat organizations and authentic teams. Taking on risk simply means we could get wounded or injured. Vulnerability and risk are the same thing. What games we've played with the words! Isn't it time we accepted the linkage? Is being vulnerable a sign of internal weakness? Only in a predatory world. Some of us have stepped out of that world and know it is easy to see the predators.

In this new work culture, what will it take for men and women to come out of hiding and use the truth about fear to reinvent themselves? For any of us who came out of the industrial model of behavior, beliefs, spirituality, management and culture, nothing short of reinvention will do.

A new game is in front of us. I can't really make a case that without you, without your getting in the game, without your definition of purpose, the world won't survive. I can state with a totally clear conscience, however, that if we are to move beyond a culture of mediocrity, we need your courage. Without our collective courage, we will never move beyond the culture we have. Without our generosity toward each other, it won't happen. And with generosity, the possibilities are endless.

What are we really frightened of? As we uplevel our work lives, step out of mediocrity, and take a stand for economic and spiritual wholeness, what do we have to be frightened of?

Plenty.

For Reflection

1. How does fear impact my life?

2. What price have I paid for the way I typically respond to fear?

3. What price have the people around me paid?

4. How can I recognize and acknowledge the distractions I use to buffer myself from fear?

5. Who are the members of my comfort tribe?

6. How can I practice complete generosity when my children, spouse, workers, coworkers, friends and I become frightened?

3

The True Path

EVERY NOBLE WORK IS AT FIRST IMPOSSIBLE.

—THOMAS CARLYLE

L ife as we have known it is over. Some of us, smarting from the experience, are asking, "So what's the point? Where's the payoff?" If we take the initiative, we can access a life far beyond the comprehension of "the working stiff." William Bridges, author of *JobShift* and director of the Center for Creative Leadership, predicts:

> *A century from now Americans will look back and marvel that we couldn't see more clearly what was happening. They will remark how fixated we were on this game of musical jobs in which, month after month, new waves of people had to drop out. They will sympathize with the suffering we were going through but will comment that it came from trying to play the game by the old rules.*[1]

---

1. William Bridges, "The End of the Job," *Fortune,* 19 Sept. 1994: 62.

Each and every one of us has a unique purpose. Hold up your thumb, look at it carefully. Is it unique? If you rob the corner store and you leave your thumbprints, are the police going to rush over and arrest your neighbor? There are millions and millions of people in this world. Most of us believe, even know, that our thumb matches no one else's. Outside of purposes for identification, what consequences does a unique thumb bring to our lives? Not much. But look at your thumbprint again. If there is such a profound difference in your thumb, what value are you giving to your life purpose? What unique meaning are you going to bring to this world?

Each of us has a unique vantage point in the world. No matter how hard I try, I could never see the world through your eyes. Each of us has a gift that comes to us so naturally that it is bigger than a job description, far more valuable than a professional title, and no one person can teach us how to use it. It is ours alone to live. The alternative is to force our way into a job description. Remember what that's like? Most of us, when looking for a job description, use words like, "I'll know it when I see it." Or we see the job description across the room and say to ourselves, *That doesn't look so bad. At least, it's not as repellent as the one I have. I can fit into that. Let's see: If I move my hand over here and force my butt over here, I could actually do this.*

As the industrial revolution breathes its last fitful gasp, we see a frightening new world with jobs marching off into history. The ground rules for successfully running a business are changing more rapidly and more chaotically every day. Stepping up to the challenge requires passion, and building a good fire is an inside job. Signing up for

yet another job description, without the internal definition of life purpose, is now insane. Remember the pre-
diction made by William Bridges: "The suffering we were
going through . . . came from trying to play the game by
the old rules."

Truth exists in our words. The lives we get emerge from
the quality of the words we use. Listen to this language
very carefully. Are we being casual about the quality,
satisfaction and meaning we are bringing to our lives?
During the industrial revolution, the words surrounding
the meaning and quality of work were casual:

- "No one loves their work."
- "It's a job."
- "You have a good job."
- "You should be happy to have a job."

In this new world, if we are going to have a rich and
fulfilled life, we need to let go of casual language regarding our life purpose until the true words of life purpose
come to us easily. For some of us, that sounds like: "I
can't believe I get paid to do this."

A journalist asked me what I love most about my
work. I replied enthusiastically, "I get to be in the presence of miracles." Prior to stepping into my life purpose,
I didn't have that experience. I suffered. Each one of us is
designed to do something better than anyone else in the
world. Until we take a stand for that, we suffer. We go to
chiropractors, doctors, resorts, television, food, alcohol,
drugs—anything to forget that our work makes us suffer,
that for some reason, the purpose in why we are here
eludes us.

I get to be present when my friend, attorney Debra Johnson, graduates from Georgetown University, moves to Los Angeles, becomes a dancer on *Solid Gold,* and after passing the bar, realizes that she is uniquely gifted to empower artists, dancers, actors, producers and authors. Debra didn't go into entertainment law because "the money's good." She realized she had a unique vantage point, a unique gift that no one had told her to use or how to use. This is key. No one will tell you to use a unique gift or how to use it. It is the one thing in your life that other people can't impose on you. No one will write a job description that perfectly describes your unique gift.

I get to be around when Boyd Willat finds a new gig. Boyd developed "The Day Runner" into the yuppie organizer that defined part of the 1980s culture. Here is someone who, through great creativity and entrepreneurial wit, built a sizable public company that produces an icon. When it sold, what next?

I get to watch when Boyd realizes he can do that again and again. From his ability to look into a market and realize what it needs, Boyd designs a pen that fits the hand of anyone who uses it. Voilà, Willat Writing Instruments. A year later, it's on display at the Museum of Modern Art. Consumers have to literally bolt these pens to their desks so people won't steal them.

We've spent 200 years trying to fit into other people's boxes, organizational job descriptions, titles and banners, and now, in this new world, we get to be ourselves. In fact, we have to commercialize being ourselves.

You have a power that comes to you so naturally no

one else is going to tell you how to do it. What is that power? What gives you such joy that you may not realize you could get paid to do it? If you are a long-term, financially successful professional, how could you use this new world to personalize your life even more? At first, this may seem impossible. Stepping outside of the previous boundaries of our existence means learning to walk again. Helen Keller did it without sight or sound. We learn to walk in a new possibility, the possibility of completely being ourselves in our work, realizing our values in our work and realizing that our real gift is as easy to use as breathing. When we're in that place, work isn't hard. Years ago, Charles Evans Hughes said: "I know hardly anyone who works too hard. I believe in hard work and long hours of work. Men do not break down from overwork, but from worry and from plunging into dissipation and efforts not aligned with their work." [2]

I remember being asked by a banking executive to give an assessment of the labor problems occurring in her organization. I responded, "Those problems have already occurred." How many people went into the banking business drawn by the promise of security? How many of us, in this culture, really wanted to do something else but bought into a promise that vanished?

Most of the people suited for a particular industry leave the moment that business starts to fail. They dust off their résumés and move on. They know they can replicate their success in better surroundings. That's basic creativity and

2. Dale Carnegie, *Dale Carnegie's Scrapbook* (New York: Simon & Schuster, 1959), 45.

adaptability. The people who are really in trouble are holding on, hanging on for dear life, hiding in their offices, hoping the human resources "death angel" won't appear. Does that sound anything like being *ourselves?*

God designed us to be ourselves, to step into a life that is unique, suits our values, includes our pleasures, and gives us a deep sense and awareness of purpose. Until we stand for that, quite simply, we suffer. This is the new revolution: to take the initiative and define what our unique purpose in the world is. If that at first seems impossible, remember that's how life usually works. A concert pianist doesn't become a concert pianist by sitting down one day and playing the Liszt E-flat Piano Concerto from memory. We learn to play a scale. We include clumsiness and mistakes and indignity because underneath the process is a greater dignity, the dignity of being ourselves, the awareness that we were meant to be a concert pianist.

I've had the privilege of seeing so many people step into their unique gift that it was a challenge to identify someone to use as a "best example." So I chose someone with a work path so unusual that we could more clearly see some of the characteristics that led her down this particular road.

Karen Golden is truly living her unique gift. Karen is a highly successful storyteller. Even I had difficulty understanding that someone could make a living being a storyteller. The fact is, Karen found her life by stepping into her purpose. Pay close attention to the events, the points of view and the natural way in which she lives.

A stage darkens in front of an audience. Many of us don't know what to expect; we've never really listened to a professional story-teller. How interesting can that be? A young woman, so authentic in her demeanor that she can't be placed in any one culture or time, walks into a pinpoint spotlight. She transforms: A midwife appears and brings new life into the world. Effortlessly, she moves from character to character—a sorcerer, a saint, an old lady watching her man die, ready to take charge of his memories. All the energy this woman expends is to make a point, to connect the members of the audience to each other through the truth in her words. The audience bursts into applause.

Karen Golden, naturally beautiful, bows and strides off the stage, picks up her baby girl from an assistant and goes home. A few days later, I'm with her in that home, a rich and welcoming environment. Her husband, a successful graphic artist, runs his business in another building on the property, and Karen has her office in the house. This allows them to work together and to spend more time with their two-year-old daughter, Hyla.

David Harder: *How did you come up with storytelling as a career?*

Karen Golden: I had tried so many different things until one day, in 1987, I was hosting a talk-radio show in Michigan, and a storyteller named Jackie Torrence performed. I was so blown away I knew that everything I had done in my life up until that point had led me to this door of storytelling.

D.H.: *What events led to that moment of truth, that moment of insight?*

K.G.: I lost my father in 1983. Dad was a cardiologist, a speaker, a well-respected educator in the field. He had a tremendous way with words. Language was extremely impor-tant to him. I adored my dad, and when he died, I felt a responsibility to keep his words, his stories alive.

I had always been committed to Judaism. I became an

educator and moved to Israel. While it was a valuable experience, I realized that wasn't it. When I returned to the United States, it was clear that I didn't want to work in education. I was really restless until that door opened in Flint.

D.H.: *Did that door lead to a free fall?*

K.G.: Absolutely! After committing to storytelling, the immediate question was:

"How do I make a living doing that? How do I get started?"

I spent my life learning what the world needed through teachers—filters. I tried so many degrees and jobs trying to do what I felt the world needed. I was never told nor was I taught how to do this. There is no voice inside of me that tells me I'm doing this "right" or "wrong." This is the unique place where something happens that is only directed by my higher self.

D.H.: *You moved from the question of "How do I get paid?" to great success with an international audience and the award of educational grants. What drove you to do it? Why are you so passionate?*

K.G.: Simply put, my art connects people. In fact, it connects me to people in ways I didn't expect.

I was once asked to perform at a retirement home in Los Angeles. I arrived after lunch and discovered that everyone was asleep. It was mortifying to speak to a group of old sleeping people. The next day, the program director called me and wanted to book another performance. "Why?" I responded. "They slept through the whole thing." The director answered that "Being awake takes on different forms, and everyone wants you to come back." And then she told me of an old man who was always neurotic about forgetting to take his medication on time. "He came to me and said he stopped being afraid. When I asked him why, he said, 'While she was here, I felt like a child again.' "

D.H.: *You have an unusually rich lifestyle. How have you integrated your life and your life work?*

K.G.: I have a wonderful life. Steve, my husband, has been a friend of mine since childhood. He proposed to me over the intercom on an airplane. When we had Hyla, we decided to run offices out of the home so she can get the attention every child needs and deserves.

D.H.: *How do we prepare children for the workplace?*

K.G.: It all boils down to child care. Life should not be kept separate from the child. We should bring the child with us. We were more tolerant of this before the era of child care centers with, commonly, a passionless adult managing our most precious responsibility. Sadly, that child is greeted at the end of the day by a tired parent. We should find a way to include our children in the best part of the day—the day itself.

D.H.: *Did the way you were raised impact the way you pursued a career?*

K.G.: Yes! When we give children high-quality attention and love, when we give them a safe place, it gives them more energy to take risks in the world. I got that from my parents, and I'm committed to providing it to my children.

The way we were raised determines what comes naturally to us as adults. Everything else requires an intervention, skills training, the release of old beliefs. Karen worked her way through an event. This event is at the beginning of every upleveling of our work lives. After observing thousands of participants upleveling their work lives, I have reached the conclusion that each one of them encounters a series of events. Each event has an obstacle attached to it. The obstacle appears in the language used to stop the process.

For example, the very first event is to choose. Nothing's going to happen if we don't choose something. Right? Author Toni Morrison, when accepting the Nobel prize for literature said, "We die. Perhaps that is the meaning of life. But we have language. And perhaps the language we use is the measure of our lives."

What is the language we use to stop choice? What are the three words we use to stop the process before we even begin? Let's try identifying those words in response to the following questions:

- What do you want to do with your life?
- What would make you happy?
- What is your purpose in life?

In our culture, we answer these inquiries with the following words: "I don't know."

Each of us has our own highly personalized truth, values and needs. Our truth exists in our words. We let ourselves off the hook from actualizing our truth with the words "I don't know." They are the verbal escape hatch.

There are different types of "not knowing." My spiritual mantra is "I don't know which end is up." This is a good form of not knowing because it keeps us open to change, coaching and mentoring possibilities. There is the "I don't know how we're going to do this" kind of not knowing. This is also good because it points out the fact that we need information. The final form of not knowing is the lie. This event protects us from life itself. "What do you want to do with your life?" "I don't know." The fact is, all of us have utterly personalized truth inside of us. If we died, they couldn't find that truth at the autopsy. The truth exists in our words. The power of the words we use gives us the power of our lives. When we use the words "I don't know" as a reaction to the possibility that life offers us, we are, quite simply, lying. The truth of what we want from our lives exists in each one of us, and it is the truth we are in charge of. This form of not knowing is the lie of the hermit crab crawling into the shell not to save it's life, but as a response to life itself. In the face of a life we could get passionate about, we turn away from that life by settling for the words "I don't know."

Karen Golden didn't settle for that. She went to Israel, she went to Flint. She tried education, she tried broadcasting. None of these clothes fit. But she didn't settle for ill-fitting clothes. She settled for her life purpose—unique, rich, personal. In doing so, she got her life. In getting our life, we set personalized standards, made real in our work. We get our truth. Work is the testing ground of that truth. It helps us differentiate between the real and the unreal.

In *Gravity and Grace,* author Simone Weil told us, "Work is needed to express what is true: also to receive what is true. We can express and receive what is false, or at least what is superficial, without any work." [3]

* What do you want to do with your life?

---

3. Edward Murphy, *The Crown Treasury of Relevant Quotations* (New York: Crown, 1978), 591.

- What would make you happy?
- What is your purpose in life?

If we continually seek refuge in the words "I don't know," if we habitually use those words as a protective shield, how could we ever get to the truth?

When we reach into that God-given place, it is unique. It is a unique expression that fits no one else's point of view. No one else tells us to do it, nor do they tell us how to do it. At best, they can give us pieces of how to do it but can never tell us to do the core. Because *we* are the core. That place always includes our values. It honors what we want out of our lives.

As we redefine the world of work, as we off-load rote and monotonous work and step into the world of value, this life purpose becomes the cornerstone not only of our success, but of our survival. How can we generate value in the world we are headed toward? After 13 years of telling thousands of people what to do and 6 years of providing a clearing for people to define their own truth, I can express only one solution: Go within. Ask the questions. Find the coach. Begin your inquiry.

How can we provide some discipline for the inquiry and turn this information into a business proposition?

We can ask the right questions. But first, we have to give up the lie. We must let go of the idea that we're in the dark. Those are the oppressive words, handed down through centuries, to keep us in the dark. Words can take us into the darkness or into the light. We are in charge of our words.

Our words determine our lives. We go within. We earnestly ask the questions:

- What am I here to contribute?
- What problem am I here to solve?
- What would bring me the greatest joy?

As the answers become defined, remember that vision is never meant to torture us. There is an old saying that I love: "pushed by the pain until we are pulled by the vision." Step through the refuge of "I don't know" into the vision. These are only words. We've stepped through those words to the next event.

As we progress through the next three chapters, we're going to label and layer each event as well as the corresponding obstacle. That way, you will see the progression from creative thought to success. But before we move on to the first event, please take a few minutes to reflect on these questions.

For Reflection

1. What am I here to contribute?

2. What problem am I here to solve?

3. What would bring me the greatest joy?

4. If I'm ready to live fully, what is my unique purpose?

4

"You Mean We Haven't Even Gotten to the Jungle and We Have to Deal with a Tribe?"

VISION. I DON'T THINK ANYTHING IS IMPOSSIBLE.

SPIRIT IS NOT BOUND BY PRECEDENT. I'M TOTALLY

UNCONCERNED ABOUT HOW IT IS GOING TO HAPPEN,

AND I'LL GO FOR IT. I'M CONSIDERED A RULE BREAKER.

—MICHAEL BECKWITH

You were born into a tribe. Each and every one of us belongs to professional, familial, social, spiritual and cultural tribes. I recently had lunch with a guy who proudly said, "I'm an academic. We're rugged individualists!" To which I responded, "Then why do you all buy shirts from the same place?"

Tribes have rigid rituals, expectations, rites of passage and language. It is a fundamental mistake to act as if we've bypassed this issue. We are, basically, a tribal culture. Tribes have a built-in mechanism designed to put us back into place when we want to step out of the tribal boundaries. They are two words (or variations of): "You're crazy."

A tribe, be it family, professional or cultural, has:

- Shared beliefs
- Shared behaviors
- Shared rituals
- Shared rites of passage
- Shared expectations
- Shared costumes

Let's take costumes as an example. If our academic had a "makeover"—Armani suit, Patek Phillipe watch, Hugo Boss shirt, Kenneth Cole shoes and a great haircut—what would the academic tribe be saying about it? "What got into him?" "Is he having a midlife crisis?" "Who does he think he is?"

When someone becomes an attorney and wants to work for a particular firm, it's considered a good idea to pay attention to the color of suit, the collar spread on the shirt and the type of shoes worn in that professional tribe. Show up without the tribal costume, and you will probably not get the job.

How about artists? What would happen if a great recording artist showed up at the recording studio wearing the suit from our aforementioned law firm? Everyone would think something was wrong.

Fitting in at the studio means wearing blue jeans, well-worn running shoes (too clean is suspicious—you are probably a dilettante) and the latest T-shirt advertising an unknown alternative rock band. No one really knows who they are, but everyone acts as if it's really great you're wearing the shirt: "Oh yeah, Gassed Frogs. They're cool."

Prior to joining any professional tribe, we belong to a tribe of origin, our family. Talk about rigid rituals and expectations! How about the mother's hierarchy of acceptable career choices? This multiple-choice option is given to many young men as they grow up. The options are based on how far up the forehead another mother's eyebrows will go when you tell her what *your* son does. Minor raise: accountant; midway up the forehead: attorney; to the hairline: a doctor. Specialties such as cardiologist provoke a natural face-lift. If a man comes from a family like that and decides he wants to be a florist, how do they respond? Some form of, "You're crazy."

When does it end? It never ends! We leave home, and we join another tribe. Los Angeles is filled with thousands upon thousands of tribes. Look through any paper with a calendar section. We've got the Korean Jogging Club, Gay Professional Parents, Survivors of Incest Who Smoke, Single and Fat—the list goes on and on. We go to work in the film industry, and it is a basic requirement to throw on an Armani sport coat and blue jeans, and carry a soft briefcase with a cellular phone glued to our ear. Another rugged individualist!

Once we fit into a tribe, we show the other tribal members that we belong by adopting the rigid rituals, costumes and expectations. Unless it's all a sham, we also adopt the beliefs of that tribe. Once we break the beliefs, the tribe reacts swiftly and strongly. Want a clue of what happens?

A participant completes one of our seminars, goes home and tells his or her spouse: "I'm going to leave my six-figure job to start a business serving the world." The spouse replies, "Are you crazy? You've got a great job."

A CEO pulls the employees aside and declares, "We're going to reengineer this business to increase customer confidence, cut costs and improve productivity. In fact, we're going to do it with the business doing well. That way we will stay ahead of the competition." The employees' reaction: "This guy's nuts."

Statement: "I'm doubling my income." Response: "Sure you are."

Invariably, we are given some form of "You're crazy." In fact, I've watched individuals make a deep-seated commitment to have a successful life, only to have the family be the very tribe that is working against that success. The tribe wouldn't know what to do if that person became happy and fulfilled. They wouldn't know whom they were dealing with anymore. They understand unhappy, unsuccessful. They won't understand happy, successful and personalized.

Getting onto our real path first happens internally. But if we are going to move beyond creative thinking, don't we have to tell someone? If we've trained our families, our professional tribes and our friends to believe that we don't like our work, that we are a "working stiff," when will they be most comfortable? Only when we show up not liking our work and as a "working stiff." If we show up as someone else, they will view it as temporal, crazy, wishful. When we get out of the box, when we move beyond our frame of reference, a framework that comes from 200 years of conditioning, the people around us will usually respond with some form of, "You're crazy."

Stepping outside of the tried and proven is frightening to the closest members of our tribe. In our families, they are frightened for us, they want us to survive. Sometimes, our friends and family members place greater stock in our surviving than in our having a full life. It isn't their fault. It's no one's fault. As members of the "modern generation," we've been wired to look for fault. In this culture, if we make a significant change or take a stand for something, people are simply going to respond, "You're crazy."

Personally, I've been terrified to take a stand against aimlessness, cynicism, contempt and resignation. If we look at individuals in our culture who have taken such stands, there has been a more horrific response than just saying, "You're crazy." Throughout history, our culture tore these individuals apart. So when our family, friends and colleagues turn to us and say, "You're crazy," it is our responsibility to retrain them. Some members of our tribe will have the awareness and flexibility to be trainable, to be coached into what we've committed to and what we consequently need. There will also be individuals who have a vested interest in the status quo.

Aspiring starving artists eventually have to get away from other starving artists if they are going to succeed. Usually, a starving artist will have a vested interest in maintaining the norm. This may sound cruel, but one commercially successful artist will be more valuable to the aspiring artist than 100 starving artists. The successful person will impart the wisdom and insight necessary to succeed, while the starving artists will simply give agreement to failure: "You poor, poor artist. I hate the casting process, too!"

I found myself in a tribe made up of baby boomers who were committed to affluence. I belonged! I kept my BMW detailed and beautiful, wore the finest clothes, dined at the best restaurants. We led vacuous lives, talking at the back of our sailboats about "the meaning of it all" when the *Challenger* shuttle exploded. I distracted myself from the sadness of having fallen into high-quality mediocrity by shopping, traveling and dining. When I left my six-figure job to do this work, virtually everyone from the old tribes thought I was nuts. "David is having a midlife crisis," they said. One of them called me up regularly, "You can't do this. You need to go back to school and get a Ph.D. in psychology. This is wrong." The people that supported me were already nuts! These were individuals who had successfully transitioned into another life. They were not captives of our culture. From my vantage point, they looked fulfilled and slightly crazy. Seven years later, I can tell you they were!

Some of the people from my old life didn't make it. When we uplevel our lives—when we take a stand for something beyond paying our bills, for a different possibility in the world—some people will find us suddenly intolerable.

What is in your life that is worth getting crazy over? Whenever we step out of the boundaries of our culture, people will find us strange, perhaps pathological. It is part of the journey, one of the events we have to step through in order to have a full, rich life. The norm with most tribes is anything but full and rich. When we take a stand for that unique and rich life purpose, we define the standards, the purpose, our role in the world. No one tells us how to do that. Our tribes will usually tell us to do something else. When we go to our tribes for evidence that we can step into this unique and rich life purpose, we usually won't find support from them.

When I was redesigning my own life, one of the standards I wrote down described the kinds of colleagues I wanted to work with. I wrote, "I only want to work with brilliant and loving people." The tribes I belonged to thought that was truly airy and fairy. There wasn't any evidence I could work with only brilliant and loving people. Today, that is my norm. If we are going to uplevel our lives, it is our responsibility to first define the lives we want to have. Then we must deal with our tribes. Otherwise, we're stuck, once again, with creative and wishful thinking.

In stepping into our life purpose, we step into a world that's moved beyond clocking in and clocking out. We step out of work that takes our life away from us and in which the weekend is the payment. We step into work that gives us life! We define the work that gives us our lives.

Pablo Picasso called work "our ultimate seduction." Most people find that statement crazy. Seduced by work? It makes work sound almost sexual, sensual, pleasurable. Exciting. Rich. Are these ideas crazy? In the old industrial work culture, it is crazy to design work that thoroughly seduces us. When we take a stand for that kind of work, the people around us will say it's crazy.

And they will say *we're* crazy if we stand for something a bit out of the norm.

"We've always done it that way before. Why are you bringing this up now?"

"Oh, her. She always comes up with harebrained ideas."

"There he goes again."

If you want to really make them nuts, *keep doing it.*

We are the most biologically dependent animal on the planet. Spiritually, there is a fundamental truth: Without the rest of us, you don't exist. Without the rest of us, there is no language, no definition, no purpose beyond running the biological entity. Quite simply, without us, you have no value. Without you, there would be no reason for me to have a purpose and deliver this work. Therefore, when we actually rebel, when we step out of the rigid expectations, rituals and belief systems of the tribe, everyone gets a bit unhinged.

Let's pose a question: How would you respond if your wife, husband, lover, spouse, best friend or sibling told you she or he was quitting everything to become a professional storyteller?

If we want to increase the probability that family members, friends, colleagues and employees will stay in our lives and actually support us, it is our responsibility, not theirs, to change the rigid rituals, expectations and belief systems of the tribe.

How many of you have had friends whine, "I really hate judgmental people"? Yet without judgment, we'd all be dead. Judgment is used to make decisions, keep us out of trouble and uphold the law. Usually, when someone tells me they hate judgmental people, what they are really asking for are permissive people. Permissive about our choices, our emotions, our desires and our expectations. We want individuals who accept us for who we are and who we are not. We get into semantic problems when we call it "judgmental." It is about acceptance.

In our culture, the norm is "low-quality rebellion." We tell everybody off and move on. That can be costly.

Spiritually, philosophically and socially, what does that accomplish? Outside of self-protection, nothing! In many cases, it's also bad business.

Most of us were taught that the world doesn't have enough. Not enough resources, money, food, even spiritual energy. In that world, our tribes never have enough, either. In the 1990s, we're realizing this may not be true. There may be enough for everybody.

Reality check: Did you just say to yourself one of the following?

- "This guy's nuts."
- "Sounds pretty New Age/woo-woo to me."
- "Wouldn't you expect this from a . . . ?"
- "California: the state that gave us crystal channelers, bean sprouts and nude encounter groups is now giving us 'Truth.'"

I am mindfully sprinkling a few ideas in here to stir things up.

Taking a stand is solely and purely our responsibility. Do you think someone walked up to me at the mall eight years ago and said, "It looks as if you are here to work in a world where people naturally live their life purpose"? No one did that. Besides, I would have responded, "That's a crock!" Eight years ago, all I wanted was a recording contract and a detailed BMW. But when I changed my direction, left the six-figure job from hell, and turned to friends and said, "I'm going to go for this," people said I was nuts.

Some of you are probably thinking, "This guy sure talks a lot about entrepreneurs. What about the rest of us?" Part of the attention we give to entrepreneurial activity is driven by the fact that much of the economic growth in our country is occurring in small to midsize companies. Today, in job searches, it is usually a mistake to limit our work options to large companies. Today, we look for work, not jobs.

Let's take a look at a few "You're crazy's" that could occur in large corporate settings. Want to hear the biggest and most common corporate "You're crazy" we've received in our work at Careermotion? Telling the truth.

We've entered a new world. In this new world, it is my conviction that companies that don't identify, promote and uphold the truth, in all sectors, will simply cease to exist. A basic truth: Change destroys liars. The world of value requires integrity and rejects everything else.

For 200 years, organizational structures from the industrial revolution were culturally covert. In many organizations, covertness is still the norm. And yet, in the world of value, such organizations are doomed to failure. They get merged and bankrupted out of existence. All too often, such companies hide from the truth behind organizational arrogance: "We're the best." "We're the leaders." "No one can touch us." For hundreds of years, telling the truth generated some form of punishment, particularly among the rank-and-file workers. Today, telling the truth is crucial to personal and organizational survival. This is a fearful change.

In bringing the imperative to identify, promote and uphold the truth, organizations had all kinds of "You're crazy" reactions:

- "This will open up a can of worms."
- "Everyone will quit."
- "We'll lose control."
- And my favorite: "How do we do that?"

Look at the process of upleveling as mechanical. The events cannot, in this world, be altered. To get out of aimlessness requires making a choice and giving up "I don't know." The reaction of your tribe with some form of "You're crazy" always happens.

If you are employed, think of a stand you could take at the office that would prompt people to offer up some form of "You're crazy." Select something that would represent an upleveling. Here are a few examples:

- "At 55, I'm going to reinvent myself and become a real team player."
- "Let's create a truth-driven business culture."
- "I'm cleaning everything up with the boss from hell."
- "I'm coming out of the closet as a Christian, a Buddhist, a gay or a New Ager." (It may not be advisable to select all of these at once.)
- "I'm submitting a proposal for a salary increase because . . ."
- "Let's create a business culture where everyone wins."

- "Now that everything's running great, let's reengineer the company so we stay with the market."
- "Let's establish a spiritually supportive work environment."

People go nuts over the spiritual references. In working with academic organizations, I recall instances where individuals went ballistic over the use of a quote from Nelson Mandela that incorporated the word *God.* Here is one such conversation between an academic and myself:

"I take grave offense to the use of this word *God.*"

"Well, how about *Buddha?*"

"No."

"How about *Christ?*"

"Never."

"How about *Black Lady in the Sky?*"

Tribes use "You're crazy" in sad attempts to ward off the inevitable: work that keeps us vibrant and alive, and a spiritualized workplace.

In the spiritualized workplace, we are rewarded with a new prize. This prize has no competition. This prize is the turning of one's head and the looking into another's eyes—eyes we have competed against and dismissed as being less right than ours; eyes that belong to the wrong political party, belief system, religion, gender or gender preference; eyes that adhere to the wrong position. We look into these eyes, expecting to encounter opposition one more time, except this time, we are faced with a terrifying and liberating truth: They are our own eyes. Sight lines connected to the same spirit.

All it takes is one moment of really seeing this one

spirit. One moment. Once that happens, there is nothing left to work against. There is only the purpose of our being present to our personal design, present to each other, present to the truth that is our lives and our work. Am I crazy?

For Reflection

1. What are a few of the positive risks I could take that would prompt my tribe to say, "You're crazy"?

2. What rituals, expectations and definitions did my family tribe give me about the nature and meaning of work?

3. Which tribal rituals, expectations and definitions no longer work?

4. If I uplevel the nature, meaning and quality of my own work, how could I inspire my tribes to support me?

5. What are some of the ungenerous ways I've responded to people when they wanted to make changes in their lives and/or take risks?

5

From the Jungle
to the World

A PERSON STARTS TO LIVE WHEN HE

CAN LIVE OUTSIDE OF HIMSELF.

—ALBERT EINSTEIN

For many of us, the next event is more threatening
than anything we've discussed thus far. We live in
a world where one of the most crucial skills for
succeeding as an adult is missing from our culture.
We used to teach this, but we don't anymore. It is
the skill of drawing attention to ourselves, particularly the ability to draw healthy attention to ourselves and to our life purpose.

To succeed in our unique life purpose, we must
define that purpose and then draw attention to it.
If we live in a culture that has forgotten how to do
that, where do we learn this skill?

In all the years I have been running employment agencies, been a career coach and led seminars, I haven't found one person who says, "If I am going to succeed, I have to draw attention to myself." Think about that. Why is it that we completely miss one of the most crucial components of success? The skill of drawing attention to ourselves is much more basic than the art of selling. It is also a critical part of the necessary skill set for successful relationships.

Once we have defined our purpose, our mission, our vision and our choice, then go to our tribe and get them to support our decision, it is time to take that purpose, mission, vision and choice into the world. To do that effectively, we need to either have or develop the skill of drawing healthy attention to ourselves.

The internal obstacle appears when we start thinking of this as some form of "They'll hurt me."

There is no such thing as fear of success. Who is really afraid of succeeding? "Fear of success" is really fear of attention. On some level, all of us know that attention—being looked at, observed, judged and criticized—is part of succeeding. I assert that this is more truthfully scary than success itself. Success is an outcome. We're not afraid of the outcome; we're afraid of the *process*. By and large, the process of getting enough people to pay attention to us, and the skill of knowing how to get people to pay attention to us, are missing from our culture.

Approximately 10 years ago, a profound movie entitled *Avalon* chronicled the arrival of an immigrant family in the United States. It's the turn of the century. Life is difficult for newcomers, and this is one committed tribe.

As each father, aunt, niece, nephew, uncle, brother and sister arrives, the family works together in making sure that each relative gets on his or her feet. They are deeply involved in each other's lives and have an active interest in each other's well-being.

Webster's Dictionary defines health as: "1. Physical and mental well-being; freedom from disease, etc. 2. Condition of body and mind. 3. A wish for one's health and happiness, as in a toast. 4. Soundness as in society or culture." So if we apply this definition to the family and look at the "healthy" family, it is a group of people who are actively committed to each other's well-being.

In *Avalon,* the family's well-being centers around a ritual: the family dinner. They gather around the table. They discuss the day. They argue over differences. They talk about the world around them. They explore what was right and what was wrong for them. They pay attention to each other. Like so many immigrant families, they become small-business owners, by opening a furniture store. One day, their entire world changes. Dad brings a miracle in the door—one of the first television sets. They are going into the business of selling this new wonder.

In one scene, the family has left the dinner table. They are transformed, transfixed, their eyes drawn from each other and glued to a glowing box, hypnotized by the world inside this device, a world that gives them no attention. Gradually, they forget to look at each other.

In the last scene, we find the perfectly groomed third generation of the family. They sit in an early 1960s, space-age living room, bathed in a green blue glow, dialogue and interaction long forgotten. They stare into space from behind their TV trays, hypnotized by the world of Lucy, Doublemint Gum and anything else this machine feeds them.

We're in trouble. The average American family communicates seven minutes a day; four of those minutes are spent arguing. That same family watches television approximately four *hours* a day. This machine doesn't feed us attention; it feeds us distraction.

Television has seduced our culture to turn our eyes from each other and become glued to a box. This mechanical action produces the single greatest skill deficit in the modern workplace: the ability to draw healthy attention to ourselves and to give healthy attention to other people.

Think about it. The norm is a few minutes of communication a day and four hours of viewing television. This "norm" doesn't include families suffering from physical, emotional or sexual violence. Those of us coming from such homes aren't just missing the skill, we're terrified of the idea.

As adults, we are thrust into the business jungle, where the unspoken rule is that to succeed, we have to draw healthy attention to ourselves. *Where do we get that?* Learning how to give healthy, high-quality attention isn't the norm. In our culture, such a state is almost abnormal. When is someone going to put the brakes on and scream, "Stop!"?

Regardless of our issues about it, the need to draw attention to ourselves doesn't go away. We commonly create all kinds of cynical reactions to this idea, and yet, that doesn't dismiss the requirement. In fact, in the new

American workplace, we find the need has grown into one of the core requirements for succeeding in our work. As we strip away layers of management in organizations, we find even the rank-and-file workers are selling services and products. Look at the phone industry. Twenty years ago, if we had told public utility workers that their industry would be deregulated and they would have to sell their products and services in a competitive world, they would have said we were nuts. The idea would have been incomprehensible. Managed care and radical changes in the health care community introduce the imperative for doctors, dentists and psychologists to sell their services. This was unexpected. Attorneys expecting collegiality, intellectually stimulating work and referred business are now competing with each other and having to sell legal services in order to survive.

We have scores of sales training and "how-to" programs for getting business. Many of these programs are ineffective because they are giving us sales techniques and not building the core skill of drawing attention to ourselves. Even though we know the "how-to" of selling, we're too frightened to use it, or our presentation is hollow and pitch oriented. We don't get the business because we don't connect with the buyer. High-quality attention gives us a high-quality "connectedness" with other people.

We've lost touch with each other. We've forgotten how to pay attention to each other. The norm is going home, flipping on the tube and kissing our mate good-night. In a culture where attention is not part of the norm, is it any wonder we stall at making a choice? Or that we master making declarations to our tribe and stop there? Ever notice how some of our friends make declarations all the time and never progress beyond the declaration?

Some of us never take responsibility for defining our life purpose because we have a subliminal awareness that after we get onto the authentic path, we're going to be required to draw attention to ourselves. Once we do commit to our life purpose and our true work, our success depends on drawing healthy attention to ourselves. With the industrial-based work culture, we had alternatives. Instead of doing work that fulfilled and satisfied us, and that required that we sell ourselves, we could do something else. We could take a rote and monotonous job where we didn't have to sell and could even hide. We survived. We got paychecks. Now, everything's changed. If we're trying to avoid this issue, forget it! We've entered the new world of "damned if you do and damned if you don't."

Many of us sought refuge from the fear of attention by taking rote, monotonous work, where we were shielded by layers of bureaucracy. Now that we are stripping away bureaucracy, selling is being imposed on most workers. Taking the job of "the working stiff" no longer provides a shield. Now everyone at the phone company is selling, and the operators are being replaced by machines. In fact, many of these large organizational cultures held the belief that it was better to get no attention than any attention at all. So, we hid.

The shield is gone. In virtually every industry and every profession, we see the emerging imperative to draw attention to ourselves. We have to sell. In flat work cultures, we become part of teams where we actually have to pay attention to each other. This is great. And for many of us, it is a healthier and terrifying new world.

Two options in the work world of today are: Get hurt quickly or starve to death slowly. When we avoid attention, we starve. Our nervous system starves. We never quite have the energy for a fulfilled and satisfying life. When we avoid attention in today's world, if we are lucky, we get by. How many employees are hiding in their offices, hoping change just goes away? When we draw attention to ourselves, we increase the potential of getting hurt. Scrutiny invites it. Higher visibility brings higher liability, and yet, there are simply no shortcuts to success. If we succeed in finding satisfaction and happiness in our work, this is the event, this is the big turning point in having such work "become real"; because when we master drawing attention to ourselves, we get fed. We become nourished. When we pay attention to our family members, when we give our children all the attention they require, they usually grow into healthy adults expecting high-quality attention as the norm.

When we build workplaces where high-quality attention to each other is fostered and supported, the workers are happy. In Robert Levering's book *A Great Place to Work,* the central theme for companies described as "great places to work" was the fact that they gave their employees high-quality recognition. We want recognition. When it doesn't exist, our nervous system doesn't function correctly. Behavioral scientist Robert Maurer points out that our nervous system needs attention for optimum health. When it doesn't exist in our workplace, we usually notice how much we don't like the environment.

Getting recognition is a learnable skill! Getting and giving attention are learnable skills! We always needed these skills for optimum health. Now, we need them to survive. As we strip away bureaucratic and management layers, teams become the primary organizational building block. To succeed in the new workplace, we must learn to tell the truth, pay attention to other team members, and draw attention to our agenda and our needs. These are all elements of collaboration, a form of high-quality attention.

One of the more profound changes I'm observing in the new workplace is the shift from competition to collaboration. It no longer works to pit workers against each other. Competition distracts our energy—energy needed to succeed with so much competition in the marketplace.

Think about the culture that could have produced this definition of collaboration: "1. To work together, particularly in some scientific or literary undertaking. 2. To cooperate with the enemy." When we take one of the single greatest skill requirements in today's workplace and our dictionary defines the skill in this way, could there be a few deep cultural issues about collaboration and attention?

Let's take a look at collaboration on the personal level:

- Where are you with the idea of drawing attention to yourself? Does it come naturally?
- Do you respond with the feeling that somehow you're going to get hurt?
- What is the quality of the attention the people in your life give you? How could that be upgraded?
- If you look at your circle and are dismayed by the low quantity and quality of attention you are getting,

what kind of people could you bring into your life who would give you high-quality attention?

Some of us grew up in homes that were quite violent. As young adults, we would often respond to attention with complete panic or by turning into aggressors ourselves. We move beyond this by upgrading the quality of people around us. These people will be fairly permissive about our moods and desires, and they will actively participate in our well-being.

We get high-quality attention because we give high-quality attention. Over time, we recover from earlier life episodes to become comfortable with attention. We can then move on to building skills in this area.

We don't learn how to have a new life alone and in a vacuum. We get a new life through the people around us. Look closely at the people around you and define the quality of attention you're getting. Remember, we are currently living in a culture where good role models are hard to find. If you want to upgrade and succeed in upgrading this area of your life, it will take initiative, new standards and a rigorous search.

Let's look at our workplace: Do we work in and/or lead a workplace where recognition and attention are two of the driving cultural forces? If not, your workplace is in trouble, and you are at risk simply by being in it. If that sounds a bit dramatic, it's because it is that dramatic. For example, experts in the field of workplace violence have extracted one primary common denominator that underscores companies at risk: an inattentive and often hostile management team. To move beyond this, several steps are required:

- Building a recognition-oriented work culture:

   Pay attention to accomplishments on a daily basis. Don't save recognition and praise for the annual performance review.

- Filling your business with mentors and coaches:

   High performance is a collaborative effort. Identify internal mentors who want to support workers in their personal development. Hire coaches who can develop specific skills needed by the organization as well as upgrade overall performance.

- Paying attention to the diverse values of your workers:

   If you see five pictures of children on an employee's desk, that person is telling you that family and children are important. If you see golf awards and mementos from tournaments, that person wants you to know that golf is valuable to him or her. Pay attention to the individual's values. If we do that, we get a stronger bond.

During inept corporate restructurings, the highly talented, creative and adaptive people leave first, leaving the company with insufficient intellectual capital for competing in the market. We call this "brain drain." Usually they leave because they are not receiving adequate attention and recognition.

Building a coaching and mentoring system into your company is a terrific way for workers to spend time together in a manner that builds the intellectual capital of the entire organization. All too often, we avoid this entire issue because of organizational aimlessness, contempt, cynicism and resignation. Usually these filters show up in some form of "This will distract us from making a profit"—a slothful response! We can build attention into our work cultures so that we actually increase the value of our workers; such environments inspire workers to contribute more. This happens when we give each person the recognition and attention they need.

What about our families? Karen Golden said, "It all boils down to child care." Our most precious responsibility is giving our children the attention they need to grow into adults who expect success and who are skilled at drawing attention to themselves. Growing into an adult who expects healthy relationships and high-quality work is the result of receiving healthy attention as a child and being taught those values. Whatever is the norm as a child becomes the norm as an adult.

If the norm in our lives is a dispassionate, even unhealthy relationship to our work, upleveling our relationship to work requires commitment, coaching, learning and modeling ourselves after people who have passionate and healthy relationships with their work. This doesn't happen while watching a sitcom. Most parenting experts advocate that we closely manage the amount of television our children see. We live in a world where even Saturday morning cartoons are so filled with violence that carrying guns has become the norm for some children.

What is happening in your home? Can we expect our children to grow up into healthy and successful adults when we turn on the television and addictively distract ourselves? When we reward ourselves for living in "work malnourishment" by centering our evenings on forgetting everything? What is to become of our children if their computers and their shows are better friends than their parents?

After working with thousands of people getting onto their authentic path, my heart aches for all the people who react to the idea of drawing attention to themselves with an automatic dismissal of the whole idea, the dismissal of finding their real life. I am saddened by a culture that settles into distraction while children, families, organizational tribes and communities move like machines: clocking in, clocking out, coming home, checking out. This is key, and it starts with you. It starts with a personal intervention. It expands with the attention we generate within our families, and it extends to our communities.

Only collectively will we move beyond the obstacle that exists with this event, the obstacle being some form of "They'll hurt me." Using this phrase doesn't necessarily signify that we had an abused childhood. It signifies the truth! Increasing our visibility increases our risk. It's hard for people to hit us if they cannot see us.

I don't believe we will be able to effect such enormous personal, tribal, organizational and community change by ourselves. Once again, this change exists only through the power of the spirit. Only by making ourselves available to that power and inspiring others to do the same will we find the ability to make such a leap. And without such a leap—without the move from distraction to attention, without the move from a culture focused on distraction to a culture focused on connectedness—what is to become of us?

Personally, I wouldn't have had the courage to bring

any of this up had I not encountered spirit. Through my encounter with spirit, I have found the power to bring attention to the spiritual agenda in front of us. Through this power, I have realized God placed us here to uniquely express the power that exists in each of us. Not a few of us. Each and every one of us has it. Through this awareness, I've taken a stand that each of us was born with a choice to stay with the status quo or to go with spirit. I've found that spirit is the very source of attention. When we connect with that power, there is no distraction as a substitute for life. Oh, we may distract to relax, but it is never an alternative to being here. For being here requires that I look at you and tell you my truth.

Being fully present to the power of spirit requires that we look at what our purpose is. Once we connect with that purpose, we find that it is so important that we simply must draw attention to it. That power exists in you and everyone around you. This is the truth.

As I looked through the community for an example of someone who demonstrates that power of drawing attention to a purpose, to a vision and a mission, Dr. Susan Love came to the forefront. Here's someone who not only made a break with the existing culture, but learned how to generate cultural change.

After becoming a breast surgeon and a member of the faculty at Harvard Medical School, Susan identified the untruths being circulated about breast cancer. She recognized the need to educate patients so they could move to empowerment vis-à-vis the medical and pharmaceutical industries. In 1990, *Dr. Susan Love's Breast Book* hit the market and gave women the information that had been so hard to get from their own doctors. A year later, she founded the National Breast Cancer Coalition, which has grown into the largest organization of breast cancer survivors in the country. In 1992, Susan left Boston to become the director of the Revlon/UCLA Breast Center, a post she resigned from just one day prior to our interview.

During our interview, we talked about the changes brought about by managed care and the opportunities Susan sees in serving the consumer. We talked about her passion for empowering the patient, about her family, and then she asked me to help her find a good piano teacher.

Courage? Here is one of the more down-to-earth individuals I've met who has taken a stand and impacted so many lives. There are members of the medical profession and the pharmaceutical industry who wish she would just go away.

David Harder: *We understand you have just resigned as director of the Revlon/UCLA Breast Center. What prompted you to do this?*

Susan Love: I came here because I wanted the chance and experience to be professorial. I wanted to teach, mentor and help youngsters, do my research and see some patients. The fact is, you can't do much programmatic work in academic medicine because all the fat has been trimmed away. There simply isn't a way to be paid if you're not seeing patients. You basically have to turn out more patients than in a private practice because you also have to pay the dean, the department, in a setting with enormous fixed overhead. That's not what I wanted to do. So I'm not going to do it.

D.H.: *With the advent of managed care, the medical profession is going through a complete "redefinement" of* *what it means to practice medicine. How do you feel about the changes?*

S.L.: Managed care has the potential to be really wonderful. The worst cases of health care I've found have been in private practices in Los Angeles. That's because the fee-for-service approach is very entrepreneurial. We do too much; we are rewarded for doing "things" even when they are of no value.

This has been the paradigm for hospitals and private doctors ingraining the notion in people that more is better, that the bigger the operation, the better. This, in fact, is not always true.

Managed care, on the other side, is saying, "We want evidence-based medicine. We want proof that what you are doing is required." This is the first time doctors have been asked to do that. They know that half the operations we are doing haven't been shown to have any benefit.

Something like a third to half of the medicines we use have never been proven to have any benefits. We just did it because we have license to do it. Some people have described medicine as a cartel, which is exactly right. Business is driving the reform because you can't reform a cartel from the inside because the stakeholders are there.

The risk of managed care is that it will go too far in the other direction, throwing the baby out with the bathwater. Women's health is not just about a Pap smear with a breast exam. We have to talk about substance abuse, domestic violence, diet and exercise. On the other hand, we're saying to the doctor, "You have 15 minutes per patient." These things are mutually exclusive, so we need to figure out a way to do both.

To do that, you have to break out of the current paradigm. In the past, everything was done by the doctor because that was the person who got paid. Now, we have the freedom to redefine that premise. Maybe the ideal option is to not have the surgeon (who wasn't a very good educator anyway) explain breast cancer.

We could use an interactive video where you input your own data, review your options and then sit down with an educator with expertise in the field. Then, you go to your physician and tell them what you want them to do.

This is what I am going to be working on: reconciling patient care, patient empowerment and evidence-based medicine, which I believe in.

D.H.: *What is this theme of patient empowerment and treating medicine as a consumer service?*

S.L.: I want to give the power of health care information back to the consumer and not have it be the province of doctors to dole out at their discretion. My upcoming hormone book is on a similar theme. The hard data about hormone replacement is minuscule. This information is controlled by the pharmaceutical companies and the medical profession, who want to make more money. I want to share what is known and what is not known with all women.

D.H.: *Where did you learn to tell the truth?*

S.L.: I don't know, but I've always been that way. My favorite compliment came from a colleague back in Boston who said, "I always think of you as the person who says, 'Hey, the emperor doesn't have any clothes.'" Being an iconoclast—that is the role I'm most proud of and I enjoy.

D.H.: *As a woman, what were some of the challenges you encountered in becoming a physician?*

S.L.: When I applied to medical school, my pre-med advisor said that I should go into biochemistry because if I went into medicine, I would be killing some young boy. It was during the Vietnam War, and he wouldn't get a deferment. The quotas for women accepted into medical school were so small that most of them responded, "Sorry, we have enough women." I put myself through Downstate [SUNY

Downstate Medical Center] in Brooklyn, and the women? We had to be better and stronger than anyone else. Only 10 percent of the class were women, and of the five top graduates, four were women. I had to go through all that sexism, which is rampant in medicine. For example, the chief of surgery at my medical school said, "We don't believe women should be surgeons." These were the people who wrote the recommendations that allowed us to move forward. It was amazing that anything happened.

When I finished and went into practice, I went through a very difficult time. Going to medical school is a socialization that is very antithetical to a lot of feminine values—one of the last male bastions. It is really being a round peg hammered into a square hole for seven years while being sleep deprived. This is not particularly fun.

It took me a while to figure out that much of the problem was the stuff they had imposed on me that didn't feel ego-syntonic, and that I could really do this my own way. After jumping through the right hoops and getting stamped on my forehead with the right stamps, [I realized] that, in fact, I could do it my way. And once I did, things got a lot easier.

D.H.: *You have such a distinct role in the world today. How did you find it?*

S.L.: I found my purpose during this time. As chief resident in surgery, I was the second woman to finish the program. I said, "I will not let them turn me into a breast surgeon." In those days, people who did breast surgery were the ones who couldn't do anything else. Either the surgeons were retiring and wanted something less stressful, or [they were] the ones who could never do the big operations. As a woman surgeon, I worried they would ghettoize and force me to become a breast surgeon. I mean, God forbid you're a woman doing hernias.

But I was sent a lot of women with breast problems, and I found that women were not getting information, were being patronized. And I started to realize that this was important. The first paper I ever wrote was in 1982—"Fibrocystic Disease and Non-Disease," a condition that didn't really exist. There wasn't a treatment because there wasn't a disease. Ever since, I've been into breaking myths. It doesn't always endear me to the group I'm part of, but I think we have to have truth tellers.

D.H.: *How did it become a political mission?*

S.L.: Much of it is being in the right place and the right time and being awake; noticing what's going on around you. When I was promoting my book in 1990, it became really clear that breast cancer was becoming politicized. I clearly remember driving with my partner, Helen, as we drove to New Hampshire and saying to her, "The time has come to politicize breast cancer, and I am perfectly situated to do it." She responded, "God, we'll never see you again."

I had academic and medical credentials as well as the trust of the women who were politicizing it. With a foot in both camps, I called some people together and was the catalyst who started it. I also said, from the beginning, "I'm not going to run this because this should be run by women with breast cancer." And now, it really doesn't matter if I'm there or not because they have taken it and run with it.

D.H.: *Do you use controversy as a tool?*

S.L.: No. I've said things like, "Breast exams are worthless. We need to get beyond breast self-exams and focus on some-thing that works." The media often reinterprets this and quotes me with, "You should never touch your breasts again!" I mean, let's move away from this song and dance, spending tons of money on shower cards when there is no evidence it makes a difference. Let's find something that works.

I've also said things like, "The current treatments for breast cancer are slash, burn and poison. Let's get beyond that and find something better." The doctors call me and say things like, "How can you say that? I'm doing the best I can." I respond, "So am I! Slashing, burning and poisoning also. It's just that this is an inadequate treatment."

I'm not about controversy. I'm about being a conscience saying, "Wait a minute. Let's go by what we know rather than what we wish were true. There are a lot of stakeholders in this, and we can get carried away."

D.H.: *Has there been a price for telling the truth?*

S.L.: Well, the question is, Is it really a price? The truth is, I'm not really at the top ranks of academic surgeons. I mean, it's interesting that I got recruited here. I've spoken to the American College of Surgeons maybe once or twice. But if you talk to the surgical leaders in this country, they would not include me because I don't play the game. Now, if you talk to the public, that's a different matter. And my power has always come from women in the public, not in the establishment.

D.H.: *How has the national visibility impacted your personal life?*

S.L.: Not a lot. I don't really acknowledge it very much. I just assume no one knows who I am. I feel it is very important to be out as a lesbian. I think that one of the problems is that if you can afford to be out, you have to be out. Every time I've been out, I've only had good responses. The first was an article about my being out in the *Boston Globe*. One of my patients walked in the door and said, "You have done the most wonderful thing for me. You gave me my son back." It so happened that her son lived in L.A. and was gay. They were estranged. He couldn't bring himself to tell her, and she sent him the article about me. She was still going to a lesbian doctor. He called her, and they got reunited.

D.H.: *Isn't the real homophobia in the gay community?*

S.L.: Absolutely! All closets are glass. I find that if you just treat this as a regular old thing and that it's no big deal, there's no problem. I think it helps to have social class. So I think those of us who do have community standing have a responsibility to be out.

But it's no big deal. We have an eight-year-old daughter. We had a landmark case with the state of Massachusetts where my lover applied for coparent adoption. Initially, they refused, so we went to the Supreme Court of Massachusetts and won. It boils down to, "This is me, this is who I am, take it or leave it."

D.H.: *What do you want our readers to understand about work?*

S.L.: I think that you need to love your work; it needs to be part of you. I mean, it shouldn't be, "Here's my life, and here's my work." It's an integral part of you, and when it stops being that way, get new work. That's what's going on with me right now. When I started feeling upset that I had an afternoon of patients to see, that meant I was burned out and needed to do something that's going to get me excited again. It's critical to keep your mind moving.

D.H.: *In preparing children to work, what do parents need to give them?*

S.L.: It begins with how we model work to children. Not as, "Oh my God, I have to go to work today, and I hate it." We model school and work as something that is fun and that we want to do. It is so important to be role models to our children.

D.H.: *Throughout this interview, I've been struck by your optimism. Is there a spiritual core to that optimism?*

S.L.: I'm generally an optimistic person. I really think I can turn anything around. I don't spend a lot of time being dreary. The other thing I want people to know is that spirituality and religion are very important. I was raised a Catholic. I'm currently in the Episcopal Church because I don't want to raise a daughter in the Catholic Church. Episcopalians think being religious and being gay is normal, and I think it's important to provide the right role model to my daughter.

I think the public is somehow surprised that I'm into spirituality, perhaps because the extreme right has taken their definition of religion and acted as if there isn't room for us. I've actually found it is harder to be out as a Christian than a lesbian.

D.H.: *With so much illness and death in your profession, how do you keep that optimistic outlook?*

S.L.: Well, you notice, I'm going to stop. I can because generally, I'm an optimistic and hopeful person. When I first started to get discouraged about how little difference I could make as a physician, I got into the politics and said, "Well, I'll make a difference by changing the whole picture."

It's not that everyone [with breast cancer] is going to die. We cure two-thirds of breast cancer. It's sitting with the one-third of the people who are going to die, and not being able to fix it and not being able to make it all better. I can do it. It's taken a lot out of me over the years, and that's why I need a break. And what happens to physicians is they either build up a wall and don't feel it, or they stop for a while.

I walked out of this interview a bit choked up. Susan Love is someone who contributes so much, lives her life as she sees fit, and has the inner health to stop and regenerate when it is needed.

Not long after our interview, I saw Susan on television, promoting her new book on hormones. When Diane Sawyer asked her about the controversy she generates, Susan smiled and said, "I'm really just a truth teller. It is so important that *someone* tells the truth."

When we look at someone who is working the realm

of "attention," Susan Love is a role model. Where does that leave us? Think about it! When you build healthy attention-drawing skills into your life, when you become generous not only in getting attention but also in giving attention, when you give full attention to the spirit inside of you and the spirit inside of each person around: What happens to your life? What happens to the people whose lives you touch?

For Reflection

1. What was the quality of attention you received as you were growing up?

2. How have your earlier experiences of getting attention impacted your ability to draw attention to yourself now?

3. How could you improve the quality of attention circulated in:
   - Your workplace?
   - Your home?
   - Your family?

4. What are the possible ramifications of drawing attention to your:
   - Career?
   - Personal needs?
   - Values?

6

Inspiring Support

M any of us would look at the title of this chapter and assume that we were going to hear a series of inspiring stories about people supporting each other so that they could succeed in each element of their life purpose. Supporting each other in having a healthy personal life, a healthy relationship to work, a vivid spiritual awareness. Actually, we're going to look at how to inspire *other* people to support *us*. It is the final event in our road map to success, the last step being to *build effective support systems.*

Do you want to know the primary reaction our participants have had to the message?

"What's that?"

A basic truth: Most people don't get what they want because they haven't taken personal responsibility to define what they want. Once we define what we want, succeeding with our purpose, our vision and our idea is solely contingent on the depth, breadth and quality of our support. Most of our clients and participants hear this and react with: "Support! Sounds good. What is it?" Many of us don't even progress to defining a choice, don't even make a commitment because we assume, in advance, that if we define it, no one will help us. Doesn't poverty start here? Poverty begins in thinking that our only recourse is to be independent, that we have to do it on our own.

I was having dinner recently with an Emmy Award-winning television producer, and we were talking about the talented people in Hollywood who make it and the talented people who don't. We were able to come up with one distinction between the two groups. The commercial failures don't believe they can afford a coach. Successful artists believe they can't afford to be without a coach. Using actors as an example, we not only find acting coaches who teach and inspire better acting, we find coaches that specialize in "the business of acting"— media coaches who prepare their acting clients for success in the public life—and coaches who help them build effective personal lives.

Six years ago, I became aware of a new possibility in my life. It dawned on me that the possibility is built into each and every one of us. Each one of us has the possibility of a fully healthy, authentic, rich, effective and joyous relationship with our work.

For years, I'd observed participants in human-potential seminars responding to cultural pressure from the seminar organizations. The pressure was to "make a difference" in the world. So we'd have people standing up and making grandiose declarations: "I'm going to heal the rain forest." "I'm going to cure cancer." "I'm going to build a new school system." Then, they'd go home. Usually, nothing happened.

The lack of results centers on two issues: The vision wasn't specific enough, and it wasn't authentic enough for the participant. So they didn't generate enough motivation to realize their vision. Even more significant was the fact each participant probably walked back into his or her noneffective support systems.

In my own life, uncovering this piece of the puzzle was a painful step. When I started Careermotion, I took a stand in the world for something greater than myself— a world where living one's unique life purpose is the cultural norm. What makes a unique life purpose different from the examples we took from the human-potential seminars is that it is deeply personal. No one tells us to do what we do. A unique life purpose is not imposed on us from our culture. It comes from within. Living our unique life purpose comes out of our existing truth, not someone else's truth. In my case, this truth emerged from the knowledge gathered as both an employment professional and an artist. It didn't emerge from someone telling me to do it. When I upleveled my purpose in the world, high-quality people were drawn to the vision. They wanted to support me.

I didn't know what to do with them!

Many of us wouldn't know what to do with support. Throughout the industrial revolution, our value was measured by how much we did, all the quotas and tasks we could complete. Today, our value is measured in how much support we can generate, how many people we can get to help us. This is a subtle yet profound change in the nature and meaning of work. Using the old work standard of survival, many of us are doing work that doesn't excite us, doesn't provoke passion, doesn't bring great meaning to our lives . . . yet we are so busy doing it. But we are not living our life purpose, and so, we suffer. We know something is missing.

In truth, there is value during this era, an era I call "chopping wood and carrying water." The moment we find our purpose, this time spent in hard work with no apparent purpose takes on tremendous value. All the learning experiences emerge as critical to our authentic role in the world. The initiative we use to find the purpose is key. Through real and earnest initiative, we find it. Once we do that, our success is contingent on the quality of the help we get.

Most of us have had no training in how to get support. For those of us who grew up in the industrial revolution work world, we often have a problem even asking for it. We rarely have an awareness of how to recruit, build, manage and reward a diverse, deep, wide, talented, brilliant and competent support system. Think about it for a moment! What would it look like if you had a diverse, deep, wide, talented, brilliant and competent support system? What if your support system was also deeply loving? What would happen to your life? What if you became part of many diverse, deep, wide, talented, brilliant, competent and loving support systems for other people?

Let's drop in on someone who gives us a terrific example of building such effective support. Marty Rogol, the president of Earth Council Foundation U.S., was one of the founders of USA for Africa and Hands Across America, two world-renowned, socially inspiring, public-awareness and fund-raising campaigns. Marty has coordinated 7 million volunteers and raised more than $100 million for charity. Throughout the national community, Marty is a natural example of inspiring others to support him. In fact, during the interview, Marty acknowledged that building support systems is so effortless for him that he sometimes feels funny about charging for it.

David Harder: *How did you progress from a law degree in 1969 to your work now?*

Marty Rogol: It was a question of timing and serendipity. In 1966, when I graduated from college, I was faced with either going on to graduate school or going to Vietnam. Grad school seemed like a much more appropriate way to spend my time. Outside of teaching, there are not many places you can take an undergraduate degree in history, so [law school] seemed like an appropriate way to go. It would give me as many options as possible, including, if I really liked it, the practice of law.

With the tenor of the times, coupled with my own politics, I decided to use the law degree in a way that could be socially beneficial. It began with a domestic poverty program known as VISTA, and I was assigned to the Neighborhood Legal Services Program in Cleveland. Being involved with any political or community activity leads to the next step, which is to understand how to get issues before the public and learn how to promote causes. This learning experience existed in my work with Ralph Nader.

Throughout all of these types of activities—whether it is working with local groups and trying to get the city council to act or with issue politics on a national level or global programs like We Are the World and Hands Across America—marketing is the underlying theme, whether you are marketing ideas or marketing products.

D.H.: *Who inspired you to work in a political arena and to do community service?*

M.R.: My family traditionally had been quite liberal. I vaguely remember stuffing envelopes for Adlai Stevenson in 1952. In my family, there was always a deep sense of activism. My aunt had been very active in politics during the Depression, and within my family, there was always this sense that such work was more interesting and got the adrenaline pumping much more than just a straight corporate type of life.

D.H.: *What did Ralph Nader give you?*

M.R.: An opportunity! An opportunity to do things at an age where lawyers took the traditional law firm route and carried partners' briefcases. I was, in fact, litigating a case against "the partner." Ralph gave me a platform where I could work on issues with his support and encouragement. I got my voice out there in a way that wouldn't have happened otherwise.

One of the enduring legacies of Nader will not only be the legislation that was passed as a result of his work on behalf of the consumer and the environment, it is the fact that he gave us an alternative career. He provided a vehicle for thousands and thousands of young lawyers to do something that was different. He also provided a place where I could really work with my beliefs without being constantly concerned with the consequences.

D.H.: *It seems as if there was this ongoing linkage between your community leadership and the entertainment industry. How did that happen?*

M.R.: There is a fun story in here. One of the last projects I completed with Nader was to create the National Public Interest Research Group, a national organization for state college students. Whenever Ralph had dealings with people involved in local, grass-roots work, he would ask me to sit in on the meetings.

One of the people who attended this meeting was the singer and songwriter Harry Chapin. Harry told us what he was doing with world hunger and expressed a desire for our assistance. We stayed in touch. After finishing my projects with Nader, Harry asked me to help him set up an organization in Washington, D.C., dealing with domestic and world hunger questions. He was very persuasive, and yet, I needed some time off and was reluctant to do it.

One night I came home—it was one of those Washington, D.C., nights where you get home at eight or nine, eat take out and turn on the TV for a little company. Harry was on the *Merv Griffin Show* sharing a story about his grandfather. Shortly before his grandfather died, he called Harry into his bedroom and said, "There are two kinds of tired, Harry. There's the tired when you have worked real hard, but you go to bed and you're real restless. And there's the good tired. That's when you go to bed and you know you fought the right fight. Oh, you may have lost, but you did the right thing. Right now, I've got a real good tired." He passed away two weeks later.

The next day, I called Harry and said I would do it.

D.H.: *What happened once you made the commitment to support him?*

M.R.: I set up the Food Policy Center in D.C. Additionally, we were involved in creating a number of projects, one of which was the World Hunger Media Awards.

Harry was a unique person. To him, "no" was a maybe, and "maybe" was a yes. He was relentless, in more ways than anyone I've ever met. His manager, Ken Kragen, also managed Kenny Rogers. Kragen got the two of them together, and Harry was constantly ·pushing Kenny to do something. Kenny Rogers, to this day, will tell you the first contribution he made was to get Harry off his back. So he gave the proceeds of a concert to the hunger effort. Through this event, Kenny became more connected to the whole vision of ending world hunger. We proposed that he sponsor the World Hunger Media Awards, which was to essentially provide a carrot for journalists to cover these issues, because journalists tend to be real good at covering events but not very good at covering a process. The whole issue of how you deal with things like long-term economic development in the third world is a process, not an event. The Awards hopefully would provide a way to generate more coverage, which, in turn, educated the public.

I got a call one morning from Harry. Kenny Rogers and his wife, Marianne, had decided they were going to underwrite the World Hunger Media Awards. Fifteen minutes later, the phone rang again—this time, from Ken Kragen. He said, "Let's not worry how the money's going to get raised, whether we do a concert or Kenny pays his own way. Let's get started and make sure this happens before the year's over." I excitedly called Harry back to tell him about the call with Kragen.

Harry had just left the house and was killed that day on the Long Island Expressway. It was as if the baton had been passed once Kenny had agreed to pick up the media awards.

D.H.: *It sounds as if Harry Chapin had a more specific gift than singer/songwriter. How would you describe that gift?*

M.R.: Harry understood as well as anybody the power of entertainment for social change and good. Before it was chic, he put himself on the line and used his celebrity for the public good as well as himself. He did a really remarkable job. He would do one concert to feed his family and the next concert to underwrite the hunger effort.

Harry Chapin was a troubadour in the true sense of the word.

D.H.: *You mentioned passing the baton to Kenny Rogers. How did Kenny use the gift?*

M.R.: To the tune of $5 million. Kenny underwrote the World Hunger Media Awards for the first five years. This came directly out of his pocket. In addition, he supported the effort with his concerts in 1984.

We did food drives at each concert, asking the audience to bring cans of food. I had worked out a deal with the local food service providers to put barrels around the venue. We wound up, over the course of 1984, collecting over 2 million pounds of food, which was locally distributed.

Kenny also helped organize both We Are the World and Hands Across America.

D.H.: *Tell us about USA for Africa and We Are the World. How did that experience impact you?*

M.R.: I consider myself one of the truly honored human beings to have been able to participate in a meaningful way. This came at a time when we were much less cynical about famine and how it's created. The outpouring, the human response, was extraordinary. People really wanted to do something. The day after the original video footage was shown on *NBC Nightly News,* people were lined up in front of the door at Oxfam in Boston to make contributions. They were there before the doors opened. That wouldn't happen today.

D.H.: *Where is our collective consciousness with hunger today?*

M.R.: Unfortunately, we've seen that warfare and power politics in Somalia and Ethiopia have played key roles in hunger. The public's instinct to [do] good is still there, but now, there is an overlay of cynicism from experiences showing that much of famine is "man produced," not "naturally produced."

Regardless of the arena, we have to move beyond constantly being seized by the negative. This makes us even more cynical, standoffish and unwilling to make commitments, particularly emotional commitments. We have to create a culture—I'm not sure how to do it—where the messages people get are positive, and not consistently negative. This is a major uphill battle!

At the core, we have media each day, armed with satellite technology, where if they can't bring us a fire at home to show on television, we can bring you one from India.

D.H.: *What role do you feel spirituality takes in all of this? Where has it taken a role in your life?*

M.R.: I think there is a great hunger within people to reach for the best in them.

I remember in the Nader days of working with all the student public-interest groups. We had a conference one year where a bunch of us were sitting around at one o'clock in the morning. There was a heated discussion taking place about the meaning of life. I was getting ready to go to bed. A young woman turned to me and asked, "How can you leave in the middle of this discussion?" One of my colleagues turned to her and said, "It's real simple. Marty's not concerned about the meaning of life. He's concerned about how to give his life meaning."

That's basically underlined my quests. To me, there is a force. I'm not quite sure what it is. You just make the most of the opportunities it gives you.

I have a very different life today. I did all the big public-interest work. Finally, I decided to learn how one has a family and deals with relationships. I got married. It's a different life with a whole new set of responsibilities. So I look for more balance in the things I do.

D.H.: *One of the common themes we're finding with the leaders we are interviewing for* The Truth About Work *is the desire to have a more balanced life. What kinds of challenges have you encountered in getting that?*

M.R.: For me, it was a bit of a shock. Simultaneously, I left the USA for Africa organization and Los Angeles, came to Florida, became a husband and a parent at the same time. Karen [Marty's wife] has a son who was 11 years old when we got married. Instead of going to meetings all over the world, I was going to Little League games. And I loved it! It was quite a change. From the perspective of personal growth, it was a valuable and important change.

D.H.: *In preparing children for careers and for work, what do you feel are the most important messages to give parents?*

M.R.: We do more good by example than by our words. I think it is most important (at least, we've found) to set basic boundaries centered on a value system. We give kids the tools to go out and do their lives, and then we let them go.

I have come to the conclusion that a key to every successful relationship is to have shared values. When that happens, things work.

D.H.: *What are you most passionate about today?*

M.R.: Two areas. One is the whole question of the environment and how it can continue to sustain any kind of lifestyle in this country and on the planet. The other is what we are doing as a society with kids.

The work I am doing with the Earth Council addresses the environment side, both internationally and domestically. It also gives us new models. We need a lot of new models. One of the things we do, in working with the Earth Council, is to develop products that are useful and that can generate revenue. This helps fund the activities that promote appropriate public policies.

D.H.: *So you are developing programs to profitize ecology?*

M.R.: I don't agree with the use of the word *profitize*. We need to generate new revenue streams. The traditional sources of funds for these kinds of activities are gone. Or, if they are not gone, they are limited in some form, either through the fact that there isn't as much money in government or the competition for dollars has expanded dramatically.

D.H.: *What do you want to accomplish with Earth Council?*

M.R.: Again, we are introducing products and new models. One of the products is an example of our intentions: We are setting up an earth-monitoring system whereby people in local communities all over the world can monitor their local environment and feed data into a major data bank. They get back information so that they know not only what is going on locally, but they can compare the data with what is going on elsewhere. This will give them valuable environmental information.

A product response to this system is the production of Earth Tool Kits, particularly for kids. This would give them the ability to go out and monitor their local environment and connect through the Internet to other kids around the world who are doing similar things. This will provide not only great data, but an educational opportunity, a communications opportunity—and, in fact, once we see the results, it will produce change.

So, to me, the way you link up things like that is the most exciting: putting people together, putting the packages together.

D.H.: *I was told that by 1992, you were responsible for raising or helping to raise over $90 million for world hunger.*

M.R.: Actually, more than that. A little over a hundred million when it was finally said and done. That was for USA for Africa.

D.H.: *How would you describe the team that helped you raise all that money?*

M.R.: It was quite extraordinary!

"We Are the World" was created through a series of connections. Harry Belafonte heard the song Bob Geldof had written called "Do They Know It's Christmas?" Belafonte had a strong reaction: "Here is this problem in Africa. The U.S. artists aren't doing anything, particularly African American artists." Harry felt that somebody needed to organize something. So he called around and someone recommended that he contact Ken Kragen. In addition to managing such stars as Harry Chapin and Kenny Rogers, Kragen was an avid supporter in the fight against world hunger.

Harry Belafonte and Ken Kragen initially talked about a concert. At that time, they didn't think a concert would generate big revenue. Geldof proved us all wrong with Live Aid when he generated over $100 million from that concert. They decided to plagiarize what he had done. Originally, it was going to be a single. At the time, Ken was also managing Lionel Richie. He talked to Lionel, who talked to Michael Jackson. They talked to Quincy Jones about producing it, and the rest is history.

It happened so quickly and with such ease! Harry called Ken a couple days before Christmas in 1984. Ken called me a day or two later and said, "Okay. Now we've got the song being written, and Quincy's agreed to produce it. Let's create an organization to manage the money." We thought, at the time, maybe we would raise $5 million. That was the projection for a single. Then one of the record company executives suggested, "Why don't you ask the artists to donate a track and create an album?" That's where we really made the money.

When Ken started talking to the artists and their managers, everybody said, "Yes!" We wound up having to turn people away. Later, we realized the phone call from Ken took place on the 23rd or 24th of December 1984. The recording session was January 28, 1985. That means between late December and the session, the song had been written, the demo tape completed and the artists pulled together. The single was released in March and the album April 1st.

So when you look at that kind of turnaround and that kind of situation, the amount of cooperation and goodwill being generated was extraordinary. We literally peaked on Good Friday of 1985, when 8,000 radio stations throughout the world simultaneously played the song. That was not organized by us. It was organized by two DJs—one in Rome, Georgia, and the other in Salt Lake City. They were working independently. They didn't know the other was doing it. Both called us, and we put them in touch with each other.

D.H.: *If everything of value comes from a collaborative effort, what are the skills of collaboration? What comes to you so naturally that you inspired all of these people to work with you?*

M.R.: I don't know. I've never really thought about it as a skill. It's like what you've just said. I agree with it completely. You can have a great idea, but unless you are able to pull the right people together with the right resources, it's a bit like if a tree falls in the forest and no one's there: Does the tree make a sound? I think you've got to understand that dynamic, but you also have to enjoy working with people.

D.H.: *You've said you haven't thought about this gift of inspiring others to work with you. Does the gift come to you as effortlessly as breathing?*

M.R.: I think that's probably correct. There's an instinct to network, to pull people together and to take the collaborative approach. I was never trained specifically in that way.

D.H.: *We find that people's unique gifts are usually the ones which they haven't been trained how to do, and they come to us without effort.*

M.R.: And then we think we're not working and there is something not quite kosher.

D.H.: *Right. It comes too easy.*

M.R.: I don't know where it comes from.

D.H.: *What do you want to leave behind?*

M.R.: As a child, the person who had the greatest impact on me was an uncle who was a doctor. He always said, "The only person who would ever know that you did any good or didn't was you." You could have done something where the outside world congratulated you and admired you, but you would know that it wasn't quite up to what you could have done. So the only place where you can get a true sense of accomplishment is internally.

I've never gotten into the bricks and mortar of what I leave behind, nor do I look to create a legacy. I think of myself as a cog in the wheel like everybody else, doing the best that I can.

D.H.: *What would you like to contribute to the world today?*

M.R.: I think more of the same.

The key element that we need at this point is to somehow figure out how to marshal the best people have to offer and to keep things as positive as we can. I saw this so clearly during everything related to We Are the World and Hands Across America. If we offer a way for people to reach to the positive side of themselves, to reach beyond themselves, they will do that. And we need to figure out more and more ways to make this available to people rather than appeal to the anger and fears, which tend to be where people go right now.

D.H.: *If you wanted to get across one message to our readers about the real value and meaning of work, what would you want them to hear?*

M.R.: Work has two components. One component is that we accomplish our purpose only partially with the talents we have. Without a mix of talents, where people work together, we really can't accomplish a whole lot.

The other side of work is that it gives our life structure—it provides our social base, the way we spend the majority of our time, how we build our relationships. And whether it's in the broadest sense of work or something else, the key factor in it is how we relate to and treat people. If we have a good idea and we relate to, inspire and treat people well, we will be successful.

Thank you, Marty!

Everything we have discussed so far in *The Truth* begins with building effective support systems. Remember how we looked at fear? Our biology requires that we get comforted when we get frightened. In appropriate circumstances, our fear requires that we get education. This requires building the right support systems for our fear. And with the very nature of work changing so rapidly, we especially need support to develop new skills. Such support systems include effective mentors, coaches and collaborators. One primary supporter is never enough.

Marty had family, aunts, uncles, Ralph Nader, Harry Chapin, Ken Kragen, Kenny Rogers and thousands of volunteers. Look at how support systems are *naturally* woven into Marty's story. If we have issues about drawing attention to ourselves and to our vision, we learn how to do that, not by ourselves, but through others. Nothing happens by ourselves! Everything occurs through collaboration, by finding the right people to help us. Why do the ceremonies for the Academy Awards, the Emmy Awards and the Pulitzer Prizes have so much trouble getting the winners to limit their speeches? Because they are so busy thanking everyone who helped them get to that podium. Success is always a collaborative effort. We never get there without asking for help from the right people.

We learn from each other. God designed our biology to require comfort, to require attention and, as we reach our highest development, to have support for each and every one of our needs and requirements. In fact, our very biological health is contingent on this kind of attention and support. Remember:

- Diverse
- Deep
- Wide
- Talented
- Brilliant
- Competent

Remember Marty. Remember your friends. Remember to thank the people who help you and inspire others to back your vision. Remember that spirit is focused on supporting others. Remember your purpose and that once you have your purpose, all success is contingent on the quality of your support. Discuss this with someone now. Find someone you can support—now.

We have completed the success path. Here is each event and obstacle that has been described since chapter 3:

Results Track

Event	Obstacle
Choice	"I don't know."
Declare it	"You're crazy."
Draw healthy attention to yourself	"They'll hurt me."
Build effective support systems	"What's that?"
Success	"Nothing."

Does any of this look familiar?

For Reflection

1. What would you build into a diverse, deep, wide, talented, brilliant and competent support system?

2. How could you generously improve the support you give others?

3. What kinds of mentors and coaches would turn your life into a greater success story?

4. What skills of collaboration do you possess, and in what ways could you inspire others by using them?

5. What is your unique life purpose?

7

The Truth About
What People Need

What do people need?

After listening to so many individuals expressing their truth, it's become quite clear and simple: People need passion. Unfortunately, after 200 years of conditioning from the industrial revolution, very few people would actually say that, despite the fact that people need it.

For most of us, work represents the biggest chunk of our lives. We spend most of our waking hours getting ready for, driving to (usually through life-threatening traffic), getting into, being at, driving home from and recovering from our work. For all of us, life ticks on, regardless of whether we are having a good time or a bad time. It ticks away regardless of whether we are passionate or bored, cynical or enthusiastic, evolving or devolving, interested or aimless. It doesn't matter; we're going to die anyway. Some of us act as if that has already happened. Take a look at the masses commuting to work. Where do you think the phrase "working stiffs" came from? It came from the same place as "the walking dead."

Without passion, without interest, without meaning, work is a bit like coming into the world and signing up for life support: We get food, air and water, but who cares? In the new world of value, not only do we have an enormous opportunity to break free from the marginal standards passed down to us by the industrial revolution; this new world requires our taking on higher standards for ourselves. It also requires that we have higher standards for our work and our relationship to work.

I'm not suggesting that any of this is easy. I don't find anyone breezing through the vast changes occurring in the world of work. In fact, I'm in awe of the individuals who are doing it without a solid spiritual base.

Regardless of the quality of our inner life, it is so important to recognize that what we believe drives our interpretations of what's happening. For example, many of us are viewing the elimination of jobs as something tragic and immoral. What if jobs are simply becoming an obsolete concept for work packaging? For example, if we don't need more bombs and fighter jets, why do politicians proudly claim, "I brought more jobs to California by pushing through this order for fighter jets"? How can someone be proud about generating something we don't need? Holding onto obsolete beliefs regarding the world, making things up to justify work that is irrelevant—this is insanity.

I remember a conversation about five years ago with an organization and development executive in the aerospace industry. California was laying off tens of thousands of workers in the defense industry. I asked her, "So when you are finished laying off 35,000 people, what are you going to do next?" She responded, "We're going to conduct market research studies, determine what the public wants, and hire the talent to create those goods and services." I responded, "Let's take a look at this for a moment. You have spent an enormous amount of money recruiting and hiring the finest high-technology talent in the world to build weapons. Now that our needs have changed, we're going to let go of this investment and start over? Did Thomas Edison create the light bulb as the result of input from a focus group?"

No! And yet, we'll get rid of these people and start over. Why not provide the means to redirect this talent and create new products and services? One that doesn't mimic other products and services in the marketplace? In truth, that organization didn't change much of anything. Five years later, they are still laying people off and are more dependent than ever on defense industry contracts to keep the doors open. This is an example of our beliefs owning us, even if they are untrue. This is insanity. This is what happens when we don't evaluate and upgrade our standards.

On a spiritual level, it is something else entirely. As the millennium draws to a close, we are being asked to wake up. As two millennia draw to a close, a floodlight is beamed on our standards, and some of us don't like what we see. Passion, creativity, adaptability, meaning and involvement: In the industrial era, these words were luxuries. In our new world, these characteristics are required. As an evolutionary leap, these characteristics are required to survive. They are no longer a luxury.

A case study of how the rank-and-file worker usually feels about work: I recall being called into the executive offices of our local government and standing in front of a receptionist in a muumuu. She didn't look up. She was reading a Barbara Cartland novel and had a sign in front of her that said: "Don't bother me, I'm having a crisis." In that moment, I came up with the idea of "citizen terminations—a wake-up call for civil servants." With this kind of interest, wouldn't you buy a voice mail system?

Another case study: I'm standing in the checkout line at the market. The cashier has a pin that says, "A Loyal Employee Since 1973." He looks about 40. I say, "Boy, you must love working here. You've been here for 20 years." He responds, "It's a job." I say, "But how do you feel about it? Do you love it?" He responds, "No one loves their work."

This poor guy demonstrates one of the most common beliefs held in our culture. If we believe no one loves his or her work, what are we sentencing ourselves to? If we believe that love affairs with our work are the domain of the privileged few, what is the best we will get?

· Can you see the risk this man is carrying into the new

workplace? Think about it: Fifteen years ago, bank tellers were indispensable. ATMs have taken so much of the work, most banks only hire part-time, benefit-free tellers. Voice-recognition systems replace telephone company operators, receptionists and customer service representatives every day. If you don't care about your work, *wake up!* Everyone working in routine and monotonous jobs is at risk. Wake up and find something that generates passion within you.

If we carry passion for our work, we naturally generate value. As Marty Rogol shared, we need new models. Today's new work model imposes the following requirements on us: purpose, attention, passion, value, creativity, unique expression, meaning and support. Aren't these the same characteristics we would look for in a love relationship? If we are spending more waking hours at work than we do with our lover or spouse, or our family, why don't we require as much fulfillment from our work?

Living powerfully in this new world is a risk-filled proposition. It is also a world filled with possibilities that didn't exist in the old world. For us "working stiffs," it is imperative to wake up to our life purpose and find passion for something. Taking that kind of stand usually means our standing up to risk and to death. By putting death out of our minds, by not being fully present in our lives, we sleep—clocking in, clocking out, until we're told our services are no longer needed. We distract ourselves from the temporal nature of life and lose the realization that every moment is filled with potential, that every moment can be either a miracle or another tick of the clock in the midst of our slumber.

Atoms are so tiny, and yet, each one has enormous power. We have that power if we choose to stand up for a full life. The alternative is to sleep through the whole thing. So many of us have been given imperatives and role models to "survive life," to get through it safely, to avoid fear and risk. And guess what? We're not going to make it! We're all going to move on from this thing we call life.

Can you see that in order to increase our probability of success, we need to "step over" the old standards? We need to step through our old beliefs, the concepts we were taught as truth and many of the definitions we were given. A robot can't produce passion for its work. This is an opportunity to stop working like a robot.

For 200 years, we were conditioned to act like machines. Now we need to differentiate ourselves from the machines because for those of us who don't uplevel everything in our work, machines become the competition. Everywhere we look, we find people failing by clinging, usually out of inappropriate reactions to fear, to obsolete work models from the industrial era. As we end a millennium, the world of work and the world of purpose reflect the enormity of our social, cultural and spiritual changes. We are in the midst of redefining life as we know it. A leap is required from each and every one of us: the leap from survival-oriented, routine-based, dispassionate work packages to our unique role in the world, the role that seduces us. How do we do that? First, we must forget everything, and we must learn the new.

I grew up as a concert pianist. For years, I studied, practiced, exercised and competed. My life was centered on discipline, discipline and, by the way, more discipline.

As an adult, I fell in love with jazz and wanted to make the transition from classical to contemporary music. I had been fortunate to study with some of the finest teachers in the world and was referred to Phil Cohen. Phil had taught some of the jazz greats. When I arrived at the studio, Phil looked like an aging beatnik, wearing sunglasses in a dark room. He motioned for me to play something. After I played for a few minutes, Phil responded, "You studied classical music?" "Yes," I said. "You must have worked with . . ." He was right "You probably did Russian exercises on the floor." Right again. "You need an emotional enema. If you are ever going to learn what it means to play living music, you have to forget everything you've learned."

Forget everything I had learned! Did this mean all the years of hard work had no value? Absolutely not. That work brought me to a turning point. Had I not mastered the work in that world, I never would have made it to the new one. Technique and skill learned over those years never abandoned me. But prior to this fundamental shift in my awareness, the technique "owned" me; I didn't "own" the technique. Learning experiences from the old world are valuable, but many of us are bound to the beliefs, behaviors and ideas of a world that no longer exists. Living in the new world requires our embracing the truth that our old world no longer owns us. Forgetting what we know first requires recognizing that everything we know is suspect. For those of us who are dependent on being "right," this can be a difficult step until we realize that the world that gave us these beliefs no longer exists.

Once I realized that, it was still difficult. My beliefs were my identity, or so I thought. You are not your beliefs. At core, you are spirit; beliefs are just concepts. The nature of spirit is everlasting change. The nature of spirit is love; the nature of love is energy, meaning and value. How is that energy and meaning defined in you? How can we inspire the individuals around us to define and pursue what's meaningful to them? How could we possibly afford to avoid these questions?

This new world of value requires that we create our revenue on meaning rather than on a one-dimensional need to survive. It means finding what we love—that hobby, that place we may have stashed away, that place we may have concealed from even ourselves because someone once said, "Don't be vulnerable or visible and most especially, don't take risks."

For those of us who settle for rote, dispassionate and monotonous work, the writing's on the wall: Robots don't give a hoot about their work, and they're easier to feed. We find that survivors in organizations that have downsized and are continuing to use industrial revolution thinking in work packages and corporate policies are becoming stressed-out machines.

Here's an example of the kind of covert and unhealthy thinking we see in such environments: "Sue [or Ed, or whoever], we think so much of you that we know you can maintain the profits in your unit without the 14 representatives you had last year." Sue, coming from the notion that "you should be happy to have a job," works 60 hours a week, never catches up, and develops physical and emotional stress. All coming from the notion that work is about survival—and nothing more.

Robots can't compete with humans who embrace passion, creativity and adaptability in their work. This gives us the three characteristics needed in the new workplace: passion, creativity and adaptability. Did our parents tell us to expect this? Usually not. Most of our parents told us to get: good jobs, benefits and predictability.

How about looking at a case study in passion? Leonard Maltin produced his first publication about movies in a vat of gelatin called a hectograph in the fifth grade. Today, he is one of the world's leading film experts, expressing his love of the movies in virtually every medium: television (*Entertainment Tonight*); books (*Leonard Maltin's Movie Video Guide—1997*); the Internet (Microsoft's *Cinemania*).

Leonard's career is one of the most pure examples of having success come to us because of the quality of our passion. It's important to recognize the distinction here. He didn't write a "career plan"; the work came to him because of the love affair he had with films. The core of Leonard's value to the marketplace is the passion that drives his knowledge, that stimulates his curiosity, that builds his talent and creativity. Leonard is in love!

The next time you see Leonard Maltin bursting with enthusiasm, remember: It's real. He is the kid in the candy store.

Leonard was a child of the first TV generation. He fell in love with old comedies and cartoons. For him, they were brand new, and he was mesmerized. The impact of *The Little Rascals, The Three Stooges* and Disney movies on Leonard was so potent that all three became subjects of books he wrote later in life. For a precocious kid, his early years are an example of someone swept away with love. In fifth grade, Leonard and a friend produced their first publication, *The Bulletin*. They first used carbons, which gave them three copies (their first circulation), and progressed to mimeograph, which gave them 35 copies. Leonard's love of movies was blossoming during this time, so the *Bulletin* became a film journal. At 13, Leonard was writing articles and columns for two fan magazines. By 15, Leonard owned one of them, *Film Fan Monthly*.

David Harder: *At 15, you were already becoming a commercial success. How did that happen?*

Leonard Maltin: First of all, let's correct a few perceptions here: I don't respond very well to the word *commercial*. None of my work came from that place or that intent. I have had this lifelong love affair with the movies. Some people refer to me, for example, as a film critic, and that isn't really the case. I'm a professional film buff, and from that place, one of the things I do is review films.

I mean, it never dawned on me to pursue being a commercial success. I had been contributing to *Film Fan Monthly* for two years. One day, the editor called me and said, "I've given five years of my life to this. I have to move on now, and I don't want it to die. Would you take it over?" I immediately responded, "Sure." He had 400 subscribers and thought a fair purchase price would be $175. Then he added, "There's $400 in the treasury, so I'm sending you a check for $225." I inherited a magazine with a subscription list, a format and money in the bank.

It always paid for itself. People thought my parents were indulging me, but they never put a nickel into it. I edited and published the magazine for nine years. I was in the 10th grade. It just overtook my life. It was the most wonderful adventure and experience. Just great!

D.H.: *Tell us about your first book.*

L.M.: In the 12th grade, an English teacher saw the magazine and became very supportive of me. She contacted me and said, "I have a friend that I want you to meet. I think the two of you will hit it off. He's an editor at Signet Books. I want you to call him and make an appointment." After school one day, I took the bus from New Jersey to New York and met him. I brought along copies of *Film Fan Monthly.* While we were chatting, he noticed the magazines on my lap and responded, "That's your magazine? I love your magazine!" This really broke the ice.

He asked me if I was familiar with a Bantam Book called *Movies on TV.* I responded that I used it and that it was pretty good. He asked, "Well, what would you do differently?" I said, "Well, I'd put in more cast names; I'd cite the director of the film; I'd put in running times, if they were cutting it; whether it's in color or black and white." I rattled all of these things off because I really did know the book very well.

He said, "Well, how would you like to do it?" I said, "You're kidding."

"No," he said. "I've been looking for someone to do a rival book. I want you to do that book."

People think I'm exaggerating when I tell this story in terms of how quickly it came together. That's exactly what happened. I mean, he hired me! He didn't have the nerve to tell anyone he had hired a 17-year-old to do these books until I produced the book. Then he asked me what I wanted to do next.

D.H.: *Who inspired you? Who were your mentors?*

L.M.: There were so many people. Before I had the credibility to interview and meet with celebrities, I wrote fan letters. Before my interest in movies grew, I wanted to be a cartoonist.

I sent fan letters to people like Charles Schulz, Chic Young and Jules Feiffer. They wrote the most wonderful responses.

Early on, I did an article on Steve Allen, and he wrote the most inspiring letter, a wonderful and very personal letter on what a good job he thought I did. He said that he thought he was qualified to judge because when he was my age, he had done a similar paper in his high school and he felt that it wasn't half as good as mine. Can you imagine being a kid and getting a letter like that? Today, I work very hard to answer my mail, especially if a kid writes it. I take extra time.

D.H.: *How did you get into television?*

L.M.: How do you get on television? Stay by the phone! In 1982, I was plugging my book in a Gene Shalit interview on the *Today* show. He was in a very loose and funny mood that day. Someone here at Paramount saw it, called the producer of *Entertainment Tonight* and asked, "You're looking for a new film critic, aren't you? I saw this guy on the *Today* show and think you ought to check him out."

A couple of days later, I got a call in New York from *Entertainment Tonight,* asking me to audition. I'd never thought about trying to get a job on television. Such a profound change in my life from a chance incident like that is astonishing to me. Certainly, this has been the biggest change in my life. It includes moving here.

I'm not trying to sound naïve or modest about this. The fact remains, there was an element of serendipity and good fortune to all of this. I was preparing myself, I was planting my seeds. So when the opportunities appeared, I was ready.

D.H.: *Pablo Picasso once described work as "our ultimate seduction." How would you coach someone to find that kind of passion?*

L.M.: First, I'd coach them to say, "Don't be afraid to admit something so personal. Don't suppress a feeling that may exist inside of you. Let it out and see if there is some way you can channel that into a career or, at the very least, a work opportunity that could become a career."

D.H.: *You have a reputation of being a nice guy. How did you keep that quality in the entertainment industry?*

L.M.: There isn't a trick to remaining a nice guy. You get back what you give out. For instance, I'm a strong believer in thank-you notes. I'm amazed at the response I get from thank-you notes. They say, "It was so nice of you, so considerate." I think it may be considerate, but it ought to be more commonplace. There was a time where people wouldn't be surprised by this; they would expect it. Show people you are paying attention by expressing congratulations on promotions and new successes. There isn't anything calculated here; it's just the right thing to do.

Being nice and honest, being a decent person has its rewards. When I met my wife, she had never known anybody who loved what they did for a living. Jobs for her had only been a means to make a living. One day, she made the rounds with me and said, "They're all such nice people." In some ways, it disturbed her! I told her that I would only work with nice people. All of my collaborators were wonderful. I had nice and easy relationships with all of them. If I had a skilled printer who was rude and awful, I'd get another printer. Quite simply, life is too short.

D.H.: *As a parent, what do you feel is most important to give children, especially so they find passion in their work?*

L.M.: First, don't watch TV during dinner. Alice and I are not perfect parents, and yet, we try real hard. We decided, early on, no TV during dinner, even if the kids plead for it. It is so important to have a time and place where we communicate with our children. Talk to your child from day one. Don't treat them like babies. Let them know what is going on around them. Encourage their participation. Stimulate their curiosity. Curiosity is the key word here. By stimulating our children to explore, to investigate and to be curious, we increase the likelihood they will find something to get excited about.

One of my pet peeves is running into workers who are not interested, who are not curious, who couldn't care less. If I go into a fast-food restaurant, I hate it when the person on the other side of the counter communicates in some way that not only do they not want to be there; they don't understand what's going on around them, either. I hate that. If you have a job, be interested in it, or stay home! If you're serving fast food, at least know what you are serving. If you're selling tickets at the theater, at least know what you are selling tickets to.

Parenting's behind this. Make sure you open your child's eyes and ears to what's going on in the world around them, what's taking place. I don't have a formula for this outside of saying: Keep talking to your children!

D.H.: *If a talented young actor or actress came to you for input on how to make it in the business, what would you tell them?*

L.M.: You better love what you are doing because it is so tough! Especially to actors, I'd say, make sure you have ways to reward yourself. Make sure you have outlets, creative self-generated outlets so that you express yourself without being dependent on the jobs, dependent on the auditions, dependent on luck and timing.

I'd never discourage someone with the drive and the passion. But I'd also encourage them to structure their career so they don't become a victim. So many actors are victimized by the casting process, bad luck, bad timing and rejection. Rejection is so much a part of the trade.

Find a way to give yourself satisfaction regularly, whether it is having an acting troupe that does plays on weekends or another creative outlet, like painting or writing. Make sure you are doing something that helps create a buffer from the slings and arrows you are going to encounter professionally.

D.H.: *What do you feel is the most important thing our readers could know about the real value and meaning of work?*

L.M.: It's hard for me to stand back and be objective because I've always loved what I do. I think that, overall, work is an expression of yourself. Work is an extension of everything that you are.

I have the ability to say that, because I started out as a writer involved in things that were interesting to me. I don't know if everyone has that opportunity. I think if you are curious and interested, you can improve any job. You can make any job better than what it says on the paper.

If you are curious and interested. Thank you, Leonard Maltin, for the passion, curiosity and interest you've brought to our world. Curiosity, interest, commitment, seduction, involvement, contribution, value, the experience of "forgetting oneself," enthusiasm, awareness, gift: If language is the measure of our lives, these are just a few of the words that are a measure of our passion.

Passion is the fuel needed to succeed in the new workplace. The fuel of predictability is long gone. Within passion, we go far enough. With passion, the motivation to identify, promote and uphold the truth is great enough for the truth to appear. For centuries, it's been said that "If you want something badly enough, the whole earth conspires to help you get it." What is it, in you, that you want so badly, the world would "conspire" to give it to you? In the world of value, "I'll do anything" is no longer enough.

We had better find something we would do anything for.

Robert Maurer compares those of us without a clear sense of purpose and vision to lizards. A lizard lies in the sun. If it gets too hot, the lizard moves. People without vision are just like that. Without a clear sense of purpose, whenever a crisis shows up, we quit. Gandhi went through tremendous discomfort, sustained by vision. Without that vision, he would have kept eating. Without vision, Gandhi might have been fat!

Work, at the end of the millennium, isn't easy. The healthy work isn't "easy." It is joyous. Finding our purpose as everything around us changes is crucial. Did we say it was also a piece of cake? Only passion pulls us through it. Remember the phrase "pushed by the pain until we are pulled by the vision." For many of us still living in the world of predictability, clocking in and clocking out, we are getting pushed by the pain. Some of us are doing that and trying not to feel it.

Where's the vision? Personalized vision generates passion. Finding our individual and unique purpose generates the fuel necessary to make it in the new work world. Each one of us has a very specific definition of work passion. For Leonard Maltin, it's the movies. For me, it's miracles. For Karen Golden, it's connecting people through stories. For Marty Rogol, it's inspiring others to become part of a vision. Susan Love is passionate about the truth. What is it for you?

Before we finish *The Truth,* we will look at ways we can define passion for ourselves. We've discussed passion as the fuel that people need. Now, what do people want?

For Reflection

1. What are you passionate about, and what are the qualities that sustain this passion?

2. What could you become passionate about?

3. What could you want so much that the world would "conspire" to give it to you?

4. What beliefs from the old world still "own" you?

8

The Truth About
What People Want

I THINK THERE IS A GREAT HUNGER WITHIN

PEOPLE TO REACH FOR THE BEST IN THEM.

—MARTY ROGOL
PRESIDENT, EARTH COUNCIL FOUNDATION U.S.

A fter discussing the world of work with so many individuals, I've come to the conclusion that most people want balance in their lives. There is a feeling that work is holding us hostage. Many of us have developed a syndrome called "losing one's life through competency." It is very common among business leaders, health care professionals, human resources executives and entrepreneurs. It is especially prevalent in jobs that are treated as "below-the-line" expenses.

Losing one's life through competency occurs when we become trained and conditioned to focus all our attention on serving others and solving other people's problems. Over time, we lose all perspective on how to serve ourselves. In that state, we lose our self-esteem, and we become unbalanced.

Take, for example, the competent human resources director who is asked to lay off 4,000 employees. That person begins the grueling process of dealing with people's anger and grief and fear. Quite often, no one asks the human resources director how he or she is fairing. That person should be "happy to have a job." Over the years, that person forgets how to take care of personal needs, inner stress and most especially, the values that need to be fulfilled in order to be happy. Losing one's life through competency is also common in large organizations that haven't come to grips with the new workplace. They don't build effective teams and implement the best technology. These companies just expect more work from fewer workers.

As we've interviewed workers, it's become very clear: We want our lives back. Some of us are parenting children for the first time, and we want to be available to meet our children's needs. We want to be present to the experience of bringing them up in the world. Some of us are in relationships in which our spouses and lovers rarely see us, and when they do, we're too tired to participate and be fully present.

We want our lives back. We want peace in our lives. We want balance in our lives. We want to live.

I'm finding that workers who are motivated, intelligent,

literate and responsible usually find work. However, in unhealthy work structures, these are often the very workers who, many times, lose their lives through the competency that is moving them ahead. This losing of one's life is fueled by a variety of scenarios. As we've discussed previously, many of us never learned how to build effective support systems. As workloads increase, we become even more consumed with meeting deadlines and completing tasks and projects, without adequate support and nourishment. The result is a "rodent wheel." Or we work for good employers and are rewarded for our competency by getting more and more responsibility. Very often, we are not getting additional support as our domain grows.

There is one other underlying scenario from the old industrial work culture. For years, profit-making organizations have separated their workers into two castes: "profit makers" and "overhead." This has to end! Building a job on the ideas that "you are overhead," "you are expendable," and "you intrude on our core business" sets up a scenario that induces work malaise, lowered accountability and apathy within the work environment. The underlying message: "You are a necessary evil."

We're going to look at the issue of balance and getting one's life back from individual and organizational vantage points. There are many contributors toward these challenges. When we create caste systems in companies, stress and dissatisfaction are natural outcomes. When we forget our own needs, stress and dissatisfaction are natural outcomes. When we settle for the basic standards given to us by the dead, and now deadly, industrial revolution—survival and predictability—stress and dissatisfaction are a given.

Let's take a look at caste systems. A dramatic shift is occurring in business. It is the phenomenon called "outsourcing." Outsourcing is taking an organizational process that is not part of our core business and turning it over to a company or individual that specializes in this kind of work. The auto industry has always outsourced advertising. Ford is in the business of building cars. It is not in the business of advertising. The ad agency handles market research, copywriting and media buying more effectively and efficiently than Ford.

The benefits of taking a job and turning it into a profit center impact everybody. Think about it for a moment: If all of the cashiers at your grocery store worked as profit-making entities, would they treat you with greater respect and professionalism? Of course! Would they expect more out of their jobs? Absolutely! The moment we place a worker in an outmoded work package where he or she is treated as overhead, that worker gets the message that he or she is more expendable than the other employees. This message, of course, undermines the individual's entire relationship to the work. For the employee, suddenly being held accountable for profits and creating value can be a big shock. Remember the receptionist at the local government office mentioned in the previous chapter? How do you think she would be acting if her job were to produce value and profit? I assert there would have been a different reception when I arrived: "Good afternoon. It's good to see you! How can I help you today?"

It is hard to have a balanced life when you are an expense. For human resources professionals, finance people and administrative workers, being treated as an expense is the norm. This has to stop.

Let's drop in on one of our friends. Kent Nethery was a highly successful human resources development executive with organizations such as Allergan and Taco Bell. Kent was well liked, taught at Pepperdine University and inspired many people to pursue organization development as a career.

Four years ago, Kent's wife, Laraine, one of Newport Beach's most successful real estate brokers, took him to dinner. She asked him to quit his job. He responded that he was doing fine. Laraine pointed out that he could probably continue working like that for the rest of his career. However, she saw an opportunity for him to have a much richer and more satisfying life.

Kent is one of those very fortunate men who married someone who is not only physically beautiful and loving, but who's also got vision, smarts and a willingness to inspire him to move beyond himself.

Today, Kent Nethery manages an international organization development firm with an extensive client base. He continues to teach at Pepperdine. There is a profound difference in the way he lives and views life now than he did before he quit his job. Today, Kent is living life to the fullest.

David Harder: *Kent, you had a successful track record directing human resources departments in multinational companies. What prompted you to leave?*

Kent Nethery: It wasn't an immediate decision. All my life, I've had terrific role models who were external consultants. When Laraine inspired me to quit my job and become an external consultant, I did so because I was attracted to the leverage and power external consultants have in bringing about change. In my experience, this transformation rarely happened without outside help.

In addition to the problems associated with being a "prophet in your own land," there are other reasons that external consultants can effect change where internal consultants cannot:

- Internal consultants are usually not valued as much as external consultants. They draw a regular salary. As such, many people within the organization are not concerned, nor are they acutely aware that they are paying for the help. In working with external consultants, employers expect more, and they typically give more power to the consultant because they are paid to deliver a specific "product."

- People who work together in an organization over a period of time get to know an internal consultant's strengths as well as his weaknesses. There is a price to pay for this.

  The client usually isn't looking for that much knowledge or information about an external worker. This allows the consultant to work more quickly and with more potency.

D.H.: *For most of your corporate career, you were a member of senior management, but you were not part of the core business, because you provided a separate service. How did that impact you?*

K.N.: In any organization, there are certain functions that are core to the company. In many ways, I was out of that loop. When we move up an organizational structure, there is more power, but it never seems to equal the power given to workers who are directly linked to the core business. I did bring power to Allergan and Taco Bell through expertise and relationships.

Despite the difference I was able to make, I always faced the obstacles of making sure I was included in the business process and reminding people that I could help with a problem or issue they may be trying to deal with.

I don't want to paint a bleak picture here. My career changes have come through recognizing the limitations in organizational structures, in jobs and in working as a "below-the-line" expense.

Different problems exist with more traditional human resources staff workers. My domain dealt with and continues to center on human resources development. Here we grow people and build value into an organization and help the organization identify how to achieve its goals.

Internally, we were seen as helpers with a function that added value to the company. Unfortunately, by not being part of the core business, we didn't ask for—nor did we expect— much in return.

D.H.: *One of the comments you made before we started is that you were spending much of your work life in meetings that had no apparent value. Tell us about that.*

K.N.: In contrast to what I've been saying, when I was doing my work, I was happiest and had an awareness of adding value to the company. The higher I got in the organization, the less time I had to do that. I was eventually spending over 70 percent of my time writing reports and completing other paperwork for meetings that weren't going anywhere and that had very little measurable value.

The problem with this many meetings is that senior management generally dictates what is going to be discussed. So much information can be sent through e-mail, memos, voice mail and the Internet. Meetings give senior management the leverage to push the priorities and protect their turf.

D.H.: *It sounds as if you felt you were idling much of the time.*

K.N.: Yes. However, along with that metaphor is the feeling that the car's resting, but the anxiety keeps mounting because of all the work that isn't getting done.

Another problem is that when we are not part of the core business, when we are an expense, we spend so much time justifying ourselves with budgets and reports that a tremendous portion of our value is removed from the organization.

For instance, I was asked to prepare a report for the company's board of directors, an important group. It was about succession and management practices. I'm a very good writer, and yet, I spent over 20 hours rewriting the report to make it politically correct—an activity that was of no value to the organization.

All of this was generating a feeling of bureaucracy that was quite discouraging.

D.H.: *Was it a crisis that moved you on?*

K.N.: Not really. I had reached my potential within the structure. When my wife pushed me, I realized I was ready to move on.

D.H.: *What happened after that conversation with your wife?*

K.N.: I started to explore options and was surprised at how many opportunities were available to me. I realized that I didn't need to rely on an organization in order to live.

D.H.: *Your wife has been an entrepreneur for some time, quite successful.*

K.N.: Yes! Her income is variable. Overall, she does very well. Laraine now puts my needs before her own. For my happiness, she was willing to put herself at risk. So many people feel trapped in emotionally stifling jobs because they fear living on variable incomes. I'm very fortunate and will always be grateful for my wife's generosity, vision and love.

Although I realized I had options and wasn't dependent on the organization, I didn't move immediately. My attitude changed in my work. I took more risks at the company. I got a promotion. There was one time I even volunteered to be laid off.

My value increased because of the awareness that I no longer needed to play it as safe.

D.H.: *Would you ever go back?*

K.N.: No. Never.

D.H.: *Why?*

K.N.: At first, I thought it was the freedom. Today, I know that isn't the case. I'm accountable to my clients now, rather than a boss. I have more options, which include moving beyond my fear of "what's next" and the need to become more disciplined. By becoming entrepreneurs, we have to replace the discipline within an organization and provide ourselves with a new inner discipline.

The primary reason why I would not return to work within a company is that I have moved from being an expense within the core of an organization to being a profit maker in my own business. In doing that, I have moved into a role where I have far more impact on my clients than when I was working internally—many times more impact.

Here are a few reasons why:

- I'm not part of the problem.
- I'm not getting jaded, feeling I'm part of a system I cannot change.
- I give what I'm paid for. When we work on a salary that is dispersed through many areas, particularly if our function doesn't generate profit, the cards are stacked against us in creating as much impact as possible.

D.H.: *Having this life experience, what would you like our readers to understand about work?*

K.N.: Let's start with a staff perspective. Is what you are doing part of the core business? If it isn't, it is difficult to demonstrate real value, measurable value to an organization. There are primary and secondary benefits.

D.H.: *It seems what you are telling us is that in today's workplace, each worker must find a way to measure and demonstrate his or her value. If we move effectively into this new workplace, demonstrating value is a key part of our success and well-being.*

K.N.: Absolutely. It has to be more than fulfilling tasks. We have to take it a step further. How is the organization going to do better? How can we add value to the organization? How can we make it a better place to work? The old standards of just doing a job or completing a task are not enough.

D.H.: *What is your life like today?*

K.N.: Much richer, more satisfying and much more diverse. Work has become an enriching and challenging part of my life. There are a few reasons for that:

- In organizations, I had enough of a track record that I could fail periodically. I think many people believe that it is "one mistake, and you are out of here." In my experience, that is usually not the case. We learn from our errors. My previous employers gave me the opportunity to make mistakes. I needed this preparation to do what I'm doing today.
- As a consultant, if I make a mistake, I'm not invited back. Fortunately, this seldom happens. But I don't have to work with difficult clients, and my work is becoming progressively more interesting.
- I have more variety, flexibility, growth experiences. Additionally, I am becoming disciplined. By and large, I'm having a great time.

The desire to find balance in our lives and in our culture has been beautifully captured by a business leader with a powerful vantage point. Sharon Bray is the corporate director of professional services and development for Lee Hecht Harrison, one of the world's leading outplacement firms. She is responsible for directing the firm's quality assurance, research and development, program design, and technology and professional development. Sharon's background includes over 20 years of experience in psychology, education, and organizational and career management consulting. Each year, her company serves thousands of clients from corporate, nonprofit and government sectors as they encounter layoffs and work transitions.

David Harder: *Tell us about your life purpose and vision.*

Sharon Bray: For the last several years, I've been absorbed with my career. This wasn't by design. It's been a very fast evolution from entering the business consulting world to being part of the senior management team. As a result, I've lost my own sense of vision and purpose. In general, my purpose is to help people learn and develop. Right now, I'm assessing my own direction. I need something more explicit because there are so many venues in which I could play that out.

Maybe it's tied to becoming 50-something: I'm going back to the drawing board. Out of all that I've done, learned and accomplished during the last 30 years of my work life, how do I redefine myself and reclaim my vision and sense of purpose? This is the question I'm in the midst of answering.

D.H.: *In the '90s, there are so many professionals asking the question, "Am I willing to sacrifice my life in order to work?" Where does that question fit into your personal assessment?*

S.B.: I started this journey about four years ago, after I gave a speech on renewal. While I gave this talk, my dad was dying from lung cancer. I was going from the [San Francisco] Bay Area to Yreka [California] to be with him, and it struck me how different our lives had become.

Dad had worked in order to support his life. It became even more clear in his dying because he had friends; he had community; he had stories; he had fullness; he had the hunting and the fishing; as well as the work. But the work was there to support this full life he had. In a few years, my life had turned into the reverse, which is, I'm "living to work." That requires some assessment.

D.H.: *You've paid a price to build a career. Where are the benefits?*

S.B.: I'm motivated by learning and by challenge. I'm one of those "high achiever" types. My satisfaction comes from getting into the next challenge, overcoming the next limit, climbing a bit farther and stretching myself.

It's not about advancement. It's all been about testing my limits. That's very important for me to distinguish. I never sat down and said, "I want to be an X when I grow up." I've merely said, "Gee, can I do that? Let me try."

D.H.: *Where did the expansion begin?*

S.B.: About 12, 13 years ago, I was living in a teeny little town in rural Nova Scotia. I was a faculty wife, married to a political scientist who was teaching at the university. As a faculty wife, there wasn't much to do outside of bridge clubs and volunteer activities. I started doing all kinds of things to stay spiritually and intellectually alive. I ran a nursery school, was a research assistant and got involved in community theater. And then my husband died suddenly in an accident.

It was a tragedy, and yet, out of that tragedy was an opportunity. I could look at leaving and growing myself, redefining what I wanted to be. That was the beginning of this intensive learning experience. I went back to school and got my doctorate. Dragging my kids with me, I entered the business world. It all happened pretty quickly.

D.H.: *What prompted you to pursue outplacement?*

S.B.: Frankly, it was an accident. I was teaching, getting my doctorate and doing a bit of freelance consulting. One day I thought, "Gee, I'd like a different challenge." I wondered if I could make it in business. "Let's try!" The most obvious route was training and development. I joined a Big Eight firm in Toronto as an instructional designer and trainer. Traveling across Canada placed demands on my ability to parent, particularly by myself. It was more than any of us could take. So, thinking it would be less stressful, I cast about again and discovered the world of outplacement consulting and counseling.

It was a natural. I'd been a counselor, a psychologist, and I knew how to do assessment. It came out of a need to help others as well as a need to be home with my daughters. That lasted a short time before it took off and became a lot of other things.

D.H.: *In working with business leaders, we keep finding this syndrome we call "losing one's life through competency." We're recognized for our competency and moved forward so quickly we don't even have time to assess how the "progress" will impact our lives.*

S.B.: As a high achiever, it can be very seductive. The people who reward you can say, "Wow! What you did was fabulous. How would you like to do this?" That's hard to turn down.

D.H.: *You have a particular vantage point in observing the world of work. How do you feel it's changing?*

S.B.: I really want to give a responsible versus pat answer. I could certainly bring up "portfolio careers," "manage your career like your own business," "constantly stay current," "benchmark your skills". . . . This is all the stuff being presented in our industry, and it's legitimate. On the other hand, there are powerful forces beneath the surface of the changes.

People are asking some very difficult questions about the disparities between the folks who have and the folks who have not. For example: As a well-educated and skilled professional, if I lost my job tomorrow, there is a high likelihood I'd be able to find another position that would support my needs fairly readily. This scenario is enhanced by my versatility. But this isn't true for many people. Often, these are the very people whose jobs are being affected the most. As a society, we haven't defined a solution for these people.

Beneath the surface of career development programs are greater societal and economic issues for North America, especially the United States. How will we provide for people? What kinds of health care benefits and social service benefits will be provided to the people who are having the greatest difficulty with the societal and economic changes impacting them?

I don't think most of us understand what's happening to us in the workplace. Technology is an important aspect of the change. I personally love technology, but there are costs to it. There is the progressive loss, even absence of community. We are losing community at work and community in the very places we live. In the midst of these changes, we have to find new ways to reach out to each other as humans, to connect and support each other emotionally. Without these changes, the workplace is losing its humanity.

Themes coming up in the workplace changes are prompting me to ask myself, *Gosh, what's the cost to me spiritually? What's the cost to me in terms of values? What's the cost in terms of my personal life and personal enrichment? What do I have to give back to the community at large if I learn how to deal with it myself?*

D.H.: *These are valuable questions for all of us to answer. In your opinion, what are the community challenges that have* *to be handled? What has to happen in addition to outplacement and other transitional services?*

S.B.: Our business provides a valuable service. But the problem we are seeing as a result of all the workplace change is bigger than our industry. We need to develop new responsibility in a number of different corners, you might say; we need to become a responsible society.

D.H.: *Your organization facilitates thousands of transitions each year. What do you feel is a success model for a high-quality work transition?*

S.B.: It is a blending of a number of things. You can never, ever make substitutes for an individual's own initiative and resourcefulness. This is a critical factor. We can throw the best resources in the world at someone, but if they don't have initiative, they're not going to use them.

It's always a partnership between what we provide and what the individual brings to the table. Often, there is the expectation that we will find that person a job and we will make that person successful. That can never happen without the will and drive of the individual.

D.H.: *Does this include the initiative of the client to be coached by a high-quality professional?*

S.B.: The field has expanded so dramatically, it's both; but it is also having access to and developing the ability to use technological resources. This is pretty critical to broadening horizons and helping people tap into new opportunities. It's no longer just using outplacement to develop a good résumé and self-marketing campaign.

At our firm, we're challenged to offer more resources to more individuals because of the enormous volume of information out there. We have to provide multiple ways for our clients to access it.

D.H.: *We've talked about the filters of aimlessness, cynicism, contempt and resignation. When you have workers come to you with those filters, how do you get past them?*

S.B.: There are other filters as well. When you've suffered a job loss, these are absolutely present for people. But there have to be other qualities for people to tap into. There has to be hope. We have to connect people to their values, the qualities that motivate them.

First, we have to encourage and allow an individual to talk about what they are feeling, openly and candidly. We have to get that out on the table; otherwise, it just festers. The next conversation is centered around "What's important to you?" There's always something, and it's where you begin the work.

D.H.: *In the Hindu law of dharma, thousands of years old, each one of us was designed to do something better than anyone else in the world. That something is a unique gift. It comes to us without effort. Do you think people are uniquely gifted?*

S.B.: I have unique gifts, but I can no longer rely on my gifts alone. We have to continually develop them, continually take them further. That is part of the challenge in the workplace today.

In moving from an industrial to knowledge revolution, what is the central message? It's: "Yes, we have gifts; we've got basic talents and strengths. But those talents and gifts will be obsolete if we don't continue to invest in them and grow them."

D.H.: *Let's address the work-packaging revolution. With options like telecommuting, job sharing, outsourcing, contingency work; with families moving to the woods with telecommuting breadwinners, we've proposed moving from a job orientation to a work orientation and then identifying the packaging best suited to our lifestyle. What are we doing to move people from traditional jobs to work packaging?*

S.B.: It's imperative. Any outplacement firm that is still preaching jobs, job descriptions and job boxes can't be competitive much longer. We absolutely have to help people understand the profound changes in the workplace. We've redesigned a number of our courses and materials, and we have created new ones that focus on the shift from jobs to work. We used to have "job-search teams." Now we have "work-search teams."

The big attitudinal and mind shift in business is "the work to be done" versus "jobs." This is an enormous change for the average American worker. We grew up believing in jobs: You get a job, a good job. This is part of our cultural heritage.

With the central theme of work versus jobs, we have to move beyond just the package the work comes in; we have to continually develop our skills and think of our talents as products we offer. With any product, we have to keep that product current, marketable and attractive to the buyer. The basic assumptions that used to drive outplacement have completely changed to reflect this new market.

D.H.: *Do you feel that work and spirituality are compatible?*

S.B.: They have to be. This is a hard issue, and I think we are only beginning to tap into it. It begins on an individual level. About a year ago, our directors of professional services worked with Bob Burnside, from the Center for Creative Leadership, to address the issues of "meaning" and "spirit" in work. We looked at the external demands on our careers and what is needed to stay employable. We also looked at our internal lives and how we were feeding and nurturing those lives.

D.H.: *Do you feel we're headed toward a spiritualized workplace?*

S.B.: I don't know if we are headed toward it. We are certainly asking questions about it. It's interesting to me that you go into a business section of any bookstore and see a lot of titles around spirituality, spirit at work, rekindling spirit, mindfulness and meaningful work, leading with soul. Much of the current and mainstream business literature centers on spirituality.

D.H.: *If you were appointed the secretary of labor, how would you describe your agenda?*

S.B.: Now, there's a question! It would tie into much of what we've discussed. There is certainly a need to help people shift their definition of "the American dream." Whatever it is, it has been redefined. So we need to answer the following questions:

1. How do we help people understand that?
2. How do we help corporations understand it?
3. How do we help people stay trained and developed?
4. Who takes responsibility for the educational piece? The educational system? The private sector? A combination of both?
5. What do we provide in retraining opportunities? What kind of resources must we create and make available to people?

It is a huge job centered on issues much deeper than simply retraining people. We have to move beyond simply retraining people to learn new skills and helping them write good résumés. There is this growing thing over there centered on community, spirit and meaning. How do we address that in our workplace?

You cannot move the heart of America without addressing this. It has to be personified in what we do, or we end up with a very cynical and unmotivated workforce.

D.H.: *We need to become a caring culture again.*

S.B.: However we do that. That is part of the agenda. Human resource professionals are certainly asking these questions because restructuring, workforce dislocation and downsizing are projected to continue.

The same old solutions—i.e., giving people an outplacement program—while those may be valuable, aren't enough.

We need to include new solutions in how we become more humane in dealing with people during these kinds of organizational changes.

D.H.: *How can parents prepare their kids for satisfying work lives?*

S.B.: I just made three presentations for an organization called Jobs for America's Graduates. This nonprofit group focuses on getting "at-risk" teenagers through high school to employment. As I worked with school counselors and job specialists, I was struck with how much I take for granted. I get state-of-the-art information on workplace trends and their impact, what's happening with competition and how that competition will impact entry-level positions. This isn't familiar information for them, and it creates a tough scenario: Kids have been given an expectation, growing up, that you get a job, have a good life. And yet, we know, on the other hand, that our kids are probably not going to be able to afford a home, a new car and all of the stuff we have today.

With all of the communications technology today, our kids are exposed in a nanosecond to all of the poverty, issues and problems in the world. I think that creates a real malaise in spirit: "What does it matter? What do I have to aim for? Why bother? Who cares?"

When I was a kid, a dream was always held out in front of me. To motivate our children, education must be multilayered, multileveled, and we need to make a real cultural shift around what we say about work, income and making a living. It means something new and different from when we were children. We have to learn, in this new world, how to inspire meaningful dreams in our children.

D.H.: *What do you feel is the greatest opportunity that faces American workers today?*

S.B.: There are opportunities that we can't even see on the screen yet, and technology is one of the things that will create those options. I think there are jobs out there, work that needs to be done, that we can't even imagine. The American workforce can help to define some of those opportunities from all of our diverse vantage points and from learning.

D.H.: *It sounds from some of the information you're getting that you may be a bit more pessimistic. You may have heard the story of the two kids with the piles of manure. For their birthdays, they both received a pile of manure. One boy threw himself down, crying, while the other boy began digging with delight, exclaiming, "If there's this much manure, there's got to be a pony somewhere!" I'm the kid looking for the pony.*

S.B.: I do know that story, and I'm like that, too.

I think we have to be, more than ever, realistic. We have to balance our hopes and wishes and opportunities. We have to look for the pony and balance it with the reality of what is happening out there because I think it's pretty serious. When I work with people and with organizations, I want to give them the facts and work with them on strategies and solutions to deal with the reality of what's in front of them.

D.H.: *What do you feel are the biggest dangers facing the American worker today?*

S.B.: Loss of spirit. I think a greater disparity between those who are making a living and those who can't. If we lose our spirit, we lose our ability to compete in today's world.

D.H.: *The last time we had a conversation, you mentioned revolutions from the marriage between Lee Hecht Harrison [outplacement] and Adia [temporary services]. Are you prepared to go on the record with any of those innovations?*

S.B.: Sure. We have a new subsidiary called Workforce Innovations, which integrates our services in a compelling way. The primary expertise they bring to the market is the development of an internal variable workforce.

Think of your contingent workforce: Adia can certainly support the traditional, contingent workers. The internal variable workforce is made up of employees from the client organization who are on payroll but are literally contracted out internally to different business units, different functions and different roles. I believe they have to stay chargeable about 80 percent of the time. There is a tracking mechanism that supports this.

An example can be found at AT&T. As employees were declared "surplus," they had an option to move into Resource Link, which was this internal and variable workforce. Now, employees began building their careers by finding the work that needed to be done!

This also gives the business unit manager an advantage in being able to evaluate the compatibility of a worker before it becomes a permanent commitment. The company community benefits by not having dislocation occurring at one end and hiring occurring at the other.

Over time, people began to choose to become part of Resource Link who hadn't even been declared surplus. Why? Because they felt it enabled them to build and develop and hone their skills much more quickly, to try new functions and opportunities.

It becomes a very strategic way to use your workforce differently. In this new model, you have a core workforce that's "permanent," an internal variable workforce and an external contingent workforce that's all part of your total staffing plan. That enables people, as they are redeployed through the organization, to have access to our other services, which include career management as well as transition services.

We are integrating our offerings this way. It's very, very exciting.

D.H.: *It sounds as if it is a terrific way to build the intellectual capital of an organization.*

S.B.: Yes. And it enables you to be very responsive to changing market demands, to operate with a much more flexible workforce, and it's also very beneficial for individuals who are a part of it.

D.H.: *One of your themes at Lee Hecht has been the emphasis on the new employment contract, where we build our employability rather than being fixated on one job. It would strike me that individuals working in that internal contingent workforce are building their employability at a much greater rate than the employees staying put in one position.*

S.B.: Well, it certainly creates career ability; there's no doubt about it. The interesting thing is, I remember the 1980s, when I read Ross Cantor's book *When Giants Learn to Dance*. There was a section in there about people needing to take a cue, in effect, from the way consultants build their own careers. Consultants go from project to project and are learning constantly as they go. An internal variable workforce has some of those same components.

D.H.: *What do you want our readers to understand about work?*

S.B.: That's a loaded question! It includes part of the evaluation I'm doing for myself.

What I would like for workers is what I would like for myself. So let me answer it personally.

The most important thing about work for me is that I have passion about it. I'm willing to struggle. I'm willing to do the hard stuff. I'm willing to do the mundane stuff if there's enough of what I love doing. Because if I love doing the work I'm engaged in: (a) it's going to be better; (b) I'm much more of a contributor to the organization; and (c) I get a lot of personal fulfillment out of it.

For me, that's most important. It sounds dreadfully clichéd to "love what you do" if you work on an assembly line. But is there some aspect of that, or is there some aspect of any work that anyone is engaged in, that provides meaning and gives you a sense of contribution? That's what I wish for every worker.

I'm particularly grateful to Sharon for being so candid with us about her own challenges. It demonstrates far more courage than simply presenting herself as the "expert" with the "answers."

If we want balance, passion and success, where do we get started?

For Reflection

1. Where could you establish more balance in your life?

2. What is the solution for establishing balance in your life?

3. If you don't work in a profit center, how could you turn it into a profit center?

4. Have you ever experienced "losing one's life through competency"? If so, what caused it?

5. How did you find yourself reacting to the discussions on outsourcing and internal variable workforces?

9

Irrevocable Happiness

HAPPINESS REQUIRES COURAGE,

PERSISTENCE, FORTITUDE, PERSEVERANCE, BRAVERY,

BOLDNESS, VALOR, VIGOR, CONCENTRATION, SOLIDITY,

SUBSTANCE, BACKBONE, GRIT, GUTS, MOXIE, NERVE,

PLUCK, RESILIENCE, SPUNK, TENACITY, TOLERANCE,

WILL POWER, CHUTZPAH AND A GOOD THESAURUS.

—JOHN-ROGER AND PETER MCWILLIAMS
THE PORTABLE LIFE 101

P assion, happiness and balance are based on your
values. They are utterly personal. What makes me
happy will not make you happy. How do we personalize it?

Let's start with going back to the example of the concert pianist and the development of artistic discipline.
First of all, can you see that when we settled for standards
of predictability and survival, satisfaction, fulfillment and
happiness came to us in the most haphazard of ways? As
an act of discipline, how much time do most of us spend
each day on defining our standards? For most of us, not
very much. Many of us can quickly express what we
don't want because we've had plenty of exercise in that
area through our random collisions with the unlikable.
Through the process of having life "dish it out" to us,
we've learned what's unpleasant and what doesn't work.

Each and every one of us has a unique blueprint—a
design, if you will—for passion. Some of us may be nuts
about golf, excited about going to the country club and
beating our handicap. Some of us don't get it. The idea
of hitting a tiny ball wearing clothes that resemble a bar-
becue cover isn't our idea of a good time. But sailing?
Nuts about it. Some of the golfers would rather have their
spleens removed than spend the day vomiting over the side
of a boat. These are two very simple examples of personal
values and needs. We start trouble when we culturalize
values and needs by making them "right" for everybody.

What about the discipline of defining happiness in our
lives and in our work? How do we define passion and
happiness in that arena?

If we say we want happiness but don't give the time
and energy toward defining it on a personalized level,
the possibility of real happiness is dismissed. It's a bit like
saying, "I want a great body" and never exercising. We're
back to creative thinking. Without defining happiness,

we get whatever our "culture pool" dishes out. By "culture pool," we mean that each and every one of us is given potential and choice. Exercising initiative, on the other hand, is up to us.

If it is true that aimlessness, contempt, cynicism and resignation are the norms in our work culture, it is also true that each one of us has the potential to move beyond them. Without using initiative and choosing to go beyond these characteristics, we are at the mercy of our culture. We float in the culture pool, where malaise is the norm.

Falling in love with our life? The probability of that happening is dramatically increased through defining the life we could fall in love with. This requires the time and energy needed to define that life.

Continued happiness comes out of redefining what is going to make us happy and developing the specific disciplines to realize that happiness. When we raise our standards, we commonly raise our standards about work and our relationship to that work.

Susan Love is in a passionate love affair with making a difference in our health. Kent Nethery is in love with producing high-quality change and value. Leonard Maltin is the joyous film buff. Sharon Bray continues to be fascinated by learning and growing, and giving that awareness to her clients. Marty Rogol gets charged up by inspiring people to support a vision. Karen Golden steps into a place where she is guided by a higher self and in so doing, connects people in a profound and powerful way. How authentic!

Raising our standards almost always means we break

away from our culture. Recently, I spoke to a client who had an extensive success record in sales and management. Everyone around her expected she would continue to grow in business. She was living their idea of a dream, yet she was unhappy. After defining that raising and caring for homeless and neglected children was what she really wanted to do, she left the corporate life. That represents a break with existing culture because it is utterly personal.

In defining what is going to make us happy, we need to determine what we could be passionate about. Leonard Maltin said, "Don't be afraid to admit something so personal." In my client's old work package, a world of meeting quotas and managing "profit and loss" centers, the world of raising homeless children was a dim, perhaps even subconscious, idea. Today she chokes up as she describes her joy in caring for three foster children as well as her own daughter. By her personalizing and defining her unique desire, did the world benefit? Did four children get the benefits of this loving woman's stepping beyond the boundaries of her culture into her unique expression of spirit, her unique life purpose?

It usually is frightening to take such a stand. And it is often embarrassing! When we make a break with the culture and become honorable to our own values, our unique gift and our unique purpose, we have to step away from a culture that didn't place great value on what is personal. Isn't it ironic that our happiness always emerges from the personal!

And there is Jack.

Jack Canfield is one of America's leading experts in the

development of human potential and personal effectiveness—a bestselling author (the *Chicken Soup for the Soul* series), seminar leader (Self-Esteem Seminars) and internationally recognized speaker. Most of us know Jack as the success story he is today.

That success came out of courage, stamina and a living, active spirituality.

Today, Jack Canfield is frequently seen on programs such as *20/20*. You will find his emotionally evocative books in virtually any bookstore in the country. He is a mentor and a friend, and it is a great pleasure to share his interview with you. Certainly, Jack Canfield's work is an antidote for cynicism, contempt, aimlessness and resignation. He is an effective argument that God designed us as instruments of joy. So before we continue discussing new standards and the pursuit of happiness, isn't it appropriate that we have a dialogue with the expert in self-esteem?

David Harder: *How did you come to put up a shingle titled Self-Esteem Expert?*

Jack Canfield: I drifted into it. It started with my own lack of self-esteem. I grew up in a dysfunctional family, with an alcoholic mother and a workaholic father. The school I went to was very competitive. They expected you to go to college. Everyone's grades were listed on a bulletin board, from the highest score to the lowest score. If you didn't do well, you were ostracized. That was where I came from.

When I entered graduate studies in psychological education at the University of Massachusetts School of Education, I started working on my own "stuff." We used to have a phrase there: "If you've got a problem, turn it into a curriculum you can teach." I started developing and teaching workshops centered on healing yourself. In fact, I became extremely interested in that whole arena.

During this same period, I moved to Chicago to become a high school teacher. While in Chicago, I met W. Clement Stone, a self-made multimillionaire and a contemporary of Napoleon Hill, the author of *Think and Grow Rich*. As I went to work with him, he began teaching me the principles of success. The first thing he taught me is, "You have to like yourself to reflect confidence."

I started using and teaching his principles in my high school history classes. They worked so well that I eventually quit teaching and went to work for Mr. Stone. Later, I became interested in the arena of the human potential movement, things like Gestalt therapy and meditation. I began integrating the personal development side with the achievement side so there would be the yin and the yang, the male and the female, the aggressive and the receptive of the personality in one's life. By then, I was pretty much hooked into the self-esteem arena.

D.H.: *So often, your name prompts faces to light up because you have touched so many people with your work. Has this impacted your feelings of self-worth?*

J.C.: I think there is a balance between one's self-esteem and self-worth being positively affected by other people's feedback, by reactions, and that deep inner knowing that you are living your true purpose and that you are right with God. This balance happens whether what you are doing is popular or not.

Most people didn't like Van Gogh's artwork at the time he was doing it. It has gone on to be worth $8 million a painting. I think, at some level, Van Gogh was probably tormented by the fact that his work wasn't accepted, but he had a deep inner drive to keep doing it. He couldn't *not* do it. One has to find that balance.

I think early on in one's career and as one is growing up in childhood, there is a dependency and need to be validated by the external world. But as one matures emotionally and spiritually, we become less and less concerned or needful of outside approval and more concerned with our own inner fulfillment.

It is always enjoyable to hear people's appreciation of my work, but it doesn't have a lot of impact on my self-worth. My self-worth is based on things that are more rock solid than people outside myself.

D.H.: *You were sharing earlier that you are in a stage in your life of needing and establishing balance. Is this a requirement for good self-esteem?*

J.C.: My self-esteem doesn't need it. My self-esteem gives me the *permission* to seek balance.

Much of my identity through the years has been attached to my work, my books and all that. But as I've grown and matured and recognized that I am a being of God, I've realized I am unfolding my own expression of spirit. I've learned there are cycles in life. There is an in-breath and an out-breath. I breathe in healing and information and growth. I exhale books, seminars, consultations and therapy with people, the things that I do for others. Not too long ago, I got overly stuck in the exhalation stage. I was working way too hard.

It was very easy to get caught up with the success of the *Chicken Soup for the Soul* books. One opportunity leads to another—the next contract, the next television appearance and the next interview. It's all very seductive. And it's all happening so fast that if I'm not careful and don't think about it, I get caught up in it.

Fortunately, I had enough time recently to become aware that I had been putting out too much energy and needed to give something back to myself.

I think if my self-image was totally attached to my work and if my self-esteem was low and I needed approval, then I would probably not be giving myself the time I need. I would be seeking external validation rather than honoring my inner impulses.

D.H.: *In the last few years, you've become a tremendous commercial success. In succeeding, what did you learn about collaboration?*

J.C.: Collaboration is important for me. I think everyone has their own row to hoe, if you will. For some people, their path may be more of a lonely path, that of a monk rather than a street minister.

For me, I want to make a huge impact, and I know that to accomplish this takes a lot of collaboration. Bill Clinton can't run the country without a whole lot of people in his cabinet and a great deal of agreement in the Congress. To achieve his goals, he needs all the people who work with him. To achieve the level of success that I wanted, I've had to work very closely with my coauthor, Mark Victor Hansen, with our publisher, Health Communications, with our public relations person, Arielle Ford. We've had to create strategic alliances with many people in the media and with numerous distribution systems.

I've found that collaboration is valuable for two reasons: One, you get to achieve more. Two, as my wife and I like to say in our couples class, "If you want to be on the fast track for spiritual growth, get married, have children and start your own business." Because if you start your own business, everything that's not clear inside of you is going to get reflected back to you from your clients, from your employees and from your vendors.

The more alliances you have, the more opportunity there is to clean up what's not clean in your internal and external relationships.

D.H.: *As I look at the theme in your work, I can't help but ask the question: What comes first, the chicken or the egg? Do we get high self-esteem first, or do we get high-quality work first?*

J.C.: They feed each other. I think if you go way back to the beginning, there is a natural desire in children to learn to walk and to learn to talk. They don't need a lot of appreciation and praise to pull that off. They just have a strong inner drive to do it. If you leave them alone, they will do their thing.

I have a six-year-old son who is a natural artist. Every day, he will spend between one and two hours—sometimes as many as four—drawing, coloring and tracing, really honing his art skills. No one has to tell him "Good job." No one has to praise him. He just wants to draw. He'll get up in the middle of a meal or stop watching television and say, "Dad, I'm going to draw now." I believe there is an internal drive toward expression that comes in at the soul level in birth. Some people seem to have higher or lower levels of that internal drive. The issue becomes a play, back and forth, between what we reinforce as parents and the prose of society. Obviously, if you are an artist and don't get any money from it, eventually you will have to do something to make a living. So society is going to press you into becoming a waiter or a bricklayer during the day, or whatever.

Initially, there is a need for positive feedback, but the deepest level of self-esteem comes primarily from the internal gratification: I did something I wanted to do, and I did it well. Eventually, you don't need someone outside of you to tell you that you did it well.

The more my self-confidence and self-esteem grow, the more I'm willing to take on bigger games and bigger challenges. I may want to do more than just start my own company. I may decide to bring together the heads of local organizations and work together to create a more positive business climate for the whole community. Or maybe I'll enroll local business leaders to take on solving the problems of hunger or homelessness. I believe that as one's sense of self expands, one can do greater and greater work.

D.H.: *Relevant to your child, I read a quote yesterday from Harry Truman: "To be a good parent, find out what your children want and then tell them to go do it."*

J.C.: Exactly. I've seen that quote, and I love it.

D.H.: *What role does spirituality play in all of this for you?*

J.C.: A huge role. I believe we are spirit in human form and that we have a purpose in being here. I believe there are some common purposes that seem to have been agreed upon, over time, by all the great religions. That is, to expand our capacity to love; to grow ourselves in wisdom; and for those who believe in reincarnation, to balance our past karma and to constantly take ourselves to higher levels of consciousness and awareness.

I also believe everybody is born with a life purpose, a destiny, something unique to express. And my point of view is that the more people act in harmony with their unique expression as well as the greater universal laws, not only are they happier, they are more at peace with themselves. I also think you produce more success in life because you are cooperating with the way things are, rather than working against nature.

I try, in my life, to tune into spirit through meditation and prayer, through participating in spiritual communities, through reading spiritual literature, and through practicing tai chi and yoga—which are things that center me and prompt me to hear the still, small voice within, the voice of God, if you will. As a result, I like to think I'm aligned with my highest self, my soul, perhaps with spirit in general. For me, aligning with God's will for my life is an important central issue in my life.

D.H.: *Michael Beckwith has said that each one of us has been designed by God to live a unique purpose and until we step into that purpose, we suffer.*

J.C.: Right. I totally agree with that.

D.H.: *If you were going to coach parents on how to raise a child to be successful and happy in the workplace, what would you tell them?*

J.C.: I would say that what one needs to do is create, within the child, a self-confidence in handling whatever shows up in their life. Instill a confidence that they can handle whatever challenges come their way in the future because they have successfully handled the ones that came in the past.

This includes encouraging the child to not run away from conflict, to not run away from challenges, to not run away from things that are hard. It means we acknowledge the child when they have taken the hard path; when they have taken a stand for their desires; when they've followed their heart; and when they've worked in ways that are harmonious with their own and their family's values. That child is going to emerge from school feeling he or she will be able to handle anything that shows up.

I think it's less important that the child has specific skills, like an ability to run a computer, although such skills are certainly valuable in today's market. Let the child know they can learn those skills if he or she needs to. The knowledge that they can respond to any challenge life gives them is far more important than any information or business skill.

Certainly, we sometimes want to push a child into things we think will be useful, but it may not be the right thing for the child. I remember the movie *The Graduate*, where they are trying to push him into plastics. "Go into plastics. That's the future!" But it obviously wasn't in alignment with Dustin Hoffman's character to go that route. One has to be unattached to what one's child is going to do.

I have three boys. I went to Harvard, a very academic route. If I had attempted to push that on my sons, I would have made them miserable. One is an artist in San Francisco. He hasn't graduated from college because he has incompletes in everything that's not art. He loves to create. My image for him when he was younger is different from what he grew up to be. So I had to constantly be asking myself, "Well, who is this child, and how can I help him be who he naturally is and express himself fully in that arena?"

My middle son is a rap singer and audio engineer, making CDs for rap artists in the [San Francisco] Bay Area—a very different scenario than the path I took. So again, I think he will be very successful. My hunch is he will someday own his own record company. But he is motivated out of his desire to do that, and not out of his need to become something I think he ought to be.

D.H.: *What is your truth about work?*

J.C.: My truth about work is that I love to work. By some people's external observation, they might call me a workaholic. Fact is, I love what I do. When I have free time, I only have about three or four things I want to do: I want to read; I want to do something athletic; I want to hang out with my family. And I want to work. So, very often on a weekend, you will find me in my office. I'm not there saying, "I wish I could be playing golf." If I were playing golf, I would probably be thinking, "Oh, I wish I were in my office working on that thing that is really fun and really challenging. I'm on a roll. I hate to leave it." So for me, my work is, literally, an expression of who I am.

I feel I'm bringing to the world greater love, greater self-acceptance, a greater belief in one's ability to achieve one's dreams and a greater tolerance of each other's unique differences. I think the world needs all of these things. But you know what? Even if the world didn't need them, I'd need to express them. So I would still do what I do!

Thank you, Jack, for being such a touchstone.

If Jack Canfield had subscribed to a cultural work standard of survival, would we have greater love, greater self-acceptance, a greater belief in one's ability to achieve one's dreams and a greater tolerance of each other's unique differences? If survival is simply a standard, what would be the ultimate upgrade? How about irrevocable happiness?

What would happen if you designed your life around a new standard of irrevocable happiness? If what you previously worked toward was survival, what would happen if your focus now was a consistent, optimum, full, rich, irrevocable happiness? Happiness you can't take away. What would it look like if you were sentenced to happiness? What if you got a lifetime sentence? What would that look like?

Quick check: Is any cynicism getting stirred up?

Start a journal. Every day, write at the head of the journal, "Irrevocable Happiness" and start writing what it means to you. As you write, you will find that your values are so personal that in many cases, they would be of very little interest to other people. For most of us, irrevocable happiness exists outside of our history, of our culture, of what people said we could have, and in some cases, outside of our logic and what we feel we deserve. Remember Leonard Maltin's words: "Don't be afraid to admit something so personal"? Well, sometimes it feels embarrassing to express it.

Our values are personal. Some of mine wouldn't interest you. Some of mine would be revolting to you. Each one of us has personal and specific standards. We only lose our permission to want what we want by surrendering to our culture's collective need to be "right." Want an example of personal and specific?

To be assured of happiness, I have to be in the company of dachshunds.

Short-legged, long-bodied, intrusive, disobedient, playful, pushy, loving and aggressive little dogs—sort of like me. How many of you expected I'd need that? Dachshunds aren't for everybody. An animal behavioralist said, "I'd rather teach a zebra to hold a lion on its head than get a dachshund to heed one command." Doesn't that just prompt you to want to go out and get one?

As I wrote in my own journal, other standards emerged. I defined that, in my work, I wanted to be surrounded by people both brilliant and loving. After 15 years in the workplace, I had no evidence this could be done, that people could be both.

I wrote that I wanted to spend more time working at home. After starting Careermotion, I remember calling a client one afternoon. She was a human resources director in the insurance industry. In the midst of our call, she asked, "I hear birds chirping in the background. Where are you?" I responded, "On my sundeck, looking at the ocean." She started ranting. "How can you get anything accomplished? Are you nuts?" I suggested we try running a little test on what we believe about work.

"So, do you believe that we need to drive through miles of hostile traffic, go into a subterranean parking garage, jump on an elevator and walk into a cubicle with fluorescent lighting in order to do our best work?" "Yes!" she said. In truth, the answer within our culture is yes.

For some of us, defining irrevocable happiness brings us to the awareness that more than anything, we want to be doing the work that our *soul* wants to do. We want to be doing the work that God designed into our soul. Many of us, as we define irrevocable happiness on a daily basis, don't dismiss our history; we make peace with our history. In so doing, the knowledge and tools and life experiences we bring from our history become active participants in the work at hand. We integrate.

So often, we don't integrate. Instead, we embrace an "either/or" belief culture. We can have one career, but not another. We can have high-quality love, but not high-quantity love. Either/or. In truth, we heal spiritually and emotionally from the quantity *and* the quality of love in our lives. In continually defining, through writing and journaling about this new standard, either/or beliefs break down. We realize the possibilities are unlimited.

As I write about work, of my awareness of spirituality and the linkage it has with life purpose, a dachshund sits on my lap and sleeps peacefully. Life is complete! But do the work and evolution end? No. Life is a process, and we advocate building joy into the present process, not waiting for it to come in the future. If that means a dog on your lap, go for it.

When we define our values and our happiness, it doesn't necessarily mean we will experience instant ecstasy. We may look at what we want and the truth of what we have, and become filled with fear. In the desire to find the work that God wants us to do, we may be looking up and sniveling, "What would you have me do, Lord?" To even ask the question means we butt up against the belief that an answer will be detestable. If that is so for us, life is already detestable.

Our life purpose exists outside of our logic, our beliefs,

our history and our limited expectations of life. The moment we take responsibility and move beyond "I don't know," we stand up to "You're crazy," "They'll hurt me" and "What's that?" This is a process of courage. The only way to get there is to take our values, the personal values that are important to us, and actualize them in our work and our lives. These values become so clear to us that we would act on them even if society didn't appreciate them. Jack Canfield did.

> *I feel I'm bringing to the world greater love, greater self-acceptance, a greater belief in one's ability to achieve one's dreams and a greater tolerance of each other's unique differences. I think the world needs all of these things. But you know what? Even if the world didn't need them, I'd need to express them. So I would still do what I do!*

Happiness is an act of discipline. How could we possibly have joy-filled lives in a chaotic world without so much as a personal definition? When we define it, remarkable things start to happen.

It often begins with discomfort. Here are a few benchmarks:

- I've watched hundreds and hundreds of people get embarrassed as they express, for the first time, that specific and personal thing that would make them happy. In our culture, unrealized vision, out-of-reach missions, purpose and values have commonly been framed as "irrelevant" and "without value." As we open our own mouths, our internalized feelings about worth and value come up. Hence, embarrassment!

- As we define irrevocable happiness, predictable thoughts show up:
  —"Won't happen."
  —"Can't happen."
  —"Impossible."
  When that happens, just remember one thing: We're making all of this up, anyway.
- We walk through the following either/or beliefs:
  —I can either have a great career and the romantic life from hell, or I can have a great romantic life and a miserable career.
  —To make this big a living, I have to give up my spirit.

By continually defining our happiness, we turn it into a discipline. We uncover opportunities that wouldn't show up because our fear would steer us someplace else or the chaos of our culture would get in the way.

Like Sharon Bray, I need to stretch and grow. In the past year, this has included licensing our seminars and service programs to make them deliverable by other people. Irrevocable happiness? I wrote down licensing and growing the business years ago. Up to the moment other people actually started delivering the programs, I was terrified. Licensing seminars sounded good on paper. It seemed like the "right" business evolution. In truth, I didn't want anyone touching my baby. What would they do with participants? What if they made mistakes? What if we designed the certification program and it didn't work? What if I wrote a book and no one read it? It's all terrifying, stepping into a world we know nothing about. We stick with defining that world until it is clear enough. We actually define it until it becomes real.

Defined dreams, linked to the right action and a strong support foundation, do come true. Today, in our work and our business, we only work with brilliant and loving collaborators, colleagues, vendors and employees. For us, that's a standard, not a dream. Without the definition, which serves, at least for me, as an "intervention in the norm," we simply get more of the contempt, cynicism, aimlessness and resignation that occur within our culture.

It comes from defining what's going to make us happy. And as we grow, we need to keep redefining it. It's like being a concert pianist who starts with learning a scale. It doesn't end there. Breakthroughs come out of a conversation. We are in charge of that conversation. When we use the conversation as a vehicle to grow our happiness, we are building the discipline of having and retaining happiness. We don't suddenly move from *pliés* to "dance as an art form" without constant exercise and practice. Exercising the discipline of happiness does lead to happiness as an "art form." Again, with initiative and practice.

Irrevocable happiness is never about living someone else's life. For one person, it's raising the homeless child. For somebody else, it's doodling, daydreaming and creating a hit cartoon series. For someone else, it's finding a cure for AIDS or holding the hand of an AIDS patient as the person dies. For another person, happiness is making a living grooming dogs. For someone else, it's awakening people's spiritual awareness or capturing the spirit of a face and adding its hidden comedy to a finished painting. For still another, it's creating a pleasantly astonishing dining experience. And for everyone, *it is precious.* I have rarely heard someone say, "What gives me irrevocable happiness is to fit in and make ends meet." There's nothing wrong with it; I've just rarely heard it.

Do you want to revolutionize your life? This is the most simple and straightforward of our exercises. Simply write out, each day, what irrevocable happiness means to you. What is your definition? What is precious to you? Your spirit will guide you.

This is the truth.

For Reflection

What would irrevocable happiness look like for you? Describe it as specifically as possible, in detail, every day.

10

"Oh, My God!"

WHAT IS ESSENTIAL IS INVISIBLE TO THE EYE.

—ANTOINE DE SAINT-EXUPÉRY

What is the truth about work?

The title put all of us on the spot. It would have been easy to write a book entitled *101 Ways to Succeed with Your Career.* But truth? Truth became a standard that exposed us to dilemmas and challenges that cannot be explained away.

In truth, all of the books, consultants, programs, seminars, how-to weekends, mission statements and good intentions are not the answer. In the end, being true to the possibility of life and the potential that exists in each of us; being true to the dilemmas that hound our culture, to the "haves" and the "have-nots", being true to ourselves—all of it comes down to being true to our source, our higher power, our God, our Buddha, our Jehovah, our Jesus, our Goddess, our light. Regardless of all the separatists and clumsy ways we try to be "right" about God, in the end, there are no shortcuts. All solutions are, ultimately, spiritual in nature.

In my opinion, the quickest and most efficient career development program is prayer. Standing in our true and unique life purpose represents a spiritual stand in the light. In that place, the truth is apparent. In that light, untruth gets burned away. It is not the easiest place to stand, but it is the true place. It is also a place of joy. When we step out of stasis—the survival-based clocking in and clocking out, the numbing, malaise-riddled, can't-wait-for-Friday, it's-a-job kind of life—and step into the light, we see God in our work. When we reach that place, it doesn't necessarily mean we quit our job on the spot. It does mean we are there for a much higher purpose than survival. We are there to express joy.

Jump!

I've been helping people jump off the crumbling ledge of the industrial revolution for a long time. But does that make me an expert? When people come to me filled with initiative to find their purpose, I know exactly what to do with them (even though I can't explain it because it comes from a higher self—a place I cannot explain): I get them to jump.

In the end, all true solutions are spiritual. Our culture is filled with dilemmas around the slipshod treatment of children, inept education, violence, drug addiction, unemployment, a media system thirsting for darkness, oppositional religious systems, corporate loyalists who feel "thrown away." We cannot use the words *the truth about work* without addressing the challenges permeating our culture.

Spiritual solutions are not the "easy route." Our relationship to routine falls away, and as we start to live outside of our culture, we may feel that we are going crazy. When we live in the truly spiritual solution, the lights are on and the work at hand is apparent. Stepping into that place is frightening and unfamiliar. It's a bit like bringing a puppy home from the pet store. We set it on the floor. The puppy starts walking in a square the same size as the cage it has lived in, and then it looks up for a moment, terrified and excited by the new world outside of the box. When we first start living in this new world, it feels like that. I just got off the phone with a client as she exclaimed, "I know this is it because I'm so unsure of myself!" What she is doing is so uniquely her that the instructions can only come from her soul.

This way of living is quite different from the world of work given to us by our culture. How do we step past cynicism, aimlessness, resignation and contempt into our spiritual work intention? How do we deal with our tribes, attracting attention and building support for something so personal that no one person can show us how to do it? Shall we hear from a few people who have done just that?

Robert Gale is the chief executive officer of the United Church of Religious Science. Also known as Science of Mind, the belief system is more of a philosophy and a way of life than a religion. It is based on the teachings of Ernest Holmes, who believed that behind all religions and spiritual teachings was one God and one spirit. Church membership exceeds 250,000 people, and the community is expected to double within the next five years.

Bob's career biography includes being a CPA with one of the Big Five accounting firms, and a senior executive with Xerox and Avon Products; a stint as an entrepreneur with multiple retail outlets; becoming a minister; and now, being a leader in the "business of religion." Bob is turning the church into a business proposition.

David Harder: *You have an unusual career biography. You were a senior executive with Avon and Xerox. Now, you are the CEO of the Church of Religious Science. How did that happen?*

Robert Gale: There has always been a sense in my life of a higher purpose. Later in life, that higher purpose manifested itself in the spiritual sense. Going way back, what has gotten me from step to step has been living within the concept of higher purpose. It may have been as simple as being in high school and a member of the football team. The higher purpose was the school, to *win* through this vehicle. Later on, it may have been a corporation. I've always had to believe in the entities that I worked for. I had to believe in their product, their integrity and their organization. That standard evolved into a spiritual life.

Where I come from now, the higher purpose is spirit, is God. For a long time, I believe, my purpose was subconscious, and that purpose has always been to serve. I learned early on that if I focused on a higher purpose, everything worked.

It worked on the levels of more money, more recognition, more promotions, the things that, at the time, were the measures of my accomplishments. During the last 10 to 15 years, the measures have changed to a sense of satisfaction, a sense that I'm making a difference and contributing in some way.

It seems now that my contributions are more global, although my complete orientation is through individual, person-to-person events. As long as I keep my willingness and openness to a higher purpose, global change happens in this very personal way.

There was a point in my life where higher purpose disappeared. During that time, it was always part of an evolution for me that required a need to change and to risk. That isn't happening anymore.

D.H.: *What did it feel like when you no longer fit into the work you were doing?*

R.G.: Like chaos and upheaval—having to make drastic changes in my life. It meant finding a different place to work. It meant leaving the corporate world and entering the entrepreneurial world. Then, it meant the shift from the entrepreneurial into the ministry, which is another form of entrepreneurship.

The move from the ministry back to an organizational role that incorporates a higher purpose, a relationship with spirit, a relationship with God—that required a major shift and more chaos in my life.

I was with Xerox and Avon Products as well as a CPA with one of the Big Five firms. I was an entrepreneur forming a partnership that built a series of retail stores. From that, I went into the ministry and back into the business world to seemingly integrate what I'm doing now, which is the business of religion.

D.H.: *How did all of this integrate into a purpose and a gift? Who inspired you and helped you to move from the business world to the spiritual world?*

R.G.: I can't really say that I have particular mentors. It has always been very much an internal process for me. Over time, there isn't one person that I can say made it happen. Without knowing it, it's been about talking to myself, listening to myself, listening to intuition, which I really call divine guidance now. At that time, it was about being introspective, paying attention to my inner voice. Hearing, "This isn't working. I'm not happy. What is it going to take?" In the early days, it was very materialistic, very "things oriented," very relationship oriented.

I've probably left more wreckage behind than others who collaborated and had mentors because I kind of "did it my way." That meant marriages and jobs that were destroyed as part of the growth process. I wouldn't change any of it because it was all necessary for me to get to this place. All provoked by listening to that inner voice.

D.H.: *When did you learn to trust that voice?*

R.G.: I learned to trust that voice as a kid by experience, trial and error. "This works. This doesn't work." Much of it came from an early childhood that was very much about survival. Relying on that voice brought me to an awareness of what, for me, was right.

In my 30s to early 40s, the practice of listening to that voice was bringing me to the concept of serving as really the only real purpose for me. In my opinion, this is the purpose for anybody who is in the world. It is the only purpose that we have, and it is a magnificent purpose. Serving is the highest purpose we can have, the highest purpose we can grasp.

D.H.: *Coming from your circumstances, who was the role model that gave you a different way to live?*

R.G.: My aunt. I was a single-parent child, didn't really know my father. Wonderful mother—still is; we're very close. But my lifeline was an aunt. I've always referred to her as my "Auntie Mame."

The attributes of an auntie Mame were given to me and have proved to be very meaningful. It was about meaningfulness, flexibility, being willing to face chaos and change. I was basically a street kid. I don't mean that in a negative way. I wasn't in gangs, but I lived in the streets. I had newspaper routes. I did whatever was necessary to survive. I was a latchkey kid, kind of on my own. This aunt was my example.

D.H.: *How would you describe the difference between people who settle for survival versus people who pursue their purpose? What are the primary distinctions?*

R.G.: For myself, it looks like an unwillingness to settle for the status quo. When we commit to higher purpose, it's always higher, so there is never any end to it. That creates the momentum. When I was very young, going into the business world and getting out with a retirement package was my ideal. That changed because it wasn't a big enough ideal.

The difference, for me, has been an unwillingness to stick with status quo. From that point, there never is enough. This has been an exciting and wonderful way to live.

D.H.: *Let's play a word game. You are handed four words and asked to coach someone to move beyond the state signified by that word. The first word is* cynicism.

R.G.: Ownership and responsibility for one's life. I would coach that person on how to understand the concepts of ownership and responsibility, and I would give them coaching on how to develop it. For example, to move our culture, we need to move beyond welfare and Social Security structures, which undermine the need for ownership and responsibility.

D.H.: *Another word:* contempt.

R.G.: It requires a shift from automatic rejection of new ideas to developing an openness to new ideas, a commitment to move beyond status quo.

D.H.: *Aimlessness.*

R.G.: Actually, I like this word. Aimlessness is a very powerful concept for me. I no longer believe that life is about goals, objectives and short-term/long-term plans. In the context of higher purpose, being open to whatever comes along, being flexible and accepting of that is a powerful way to live.

I can't outthink what the higher purpose is going to be. I need to be aimless so I'm not limiting myself to that higher purpose. Being aimless is a very powerful attribute.

D.H.: *Actually, within our semantics, what you've described is anything but aimless. An aimless person would never have the spiritual commitment to sit down, be open and wait for input.*
What about resignation?

R.G.: To me, that immediately becomes compromise. That's a sad state that happens in the workplace. Resignation in the workplace happens when people believe they need to do that in order to survive—not speaking up, not expressing themselves, not communicating.

Those are the words that come up in my mind. Resignation disappears in the face of individual ownership, ownership in what they do and in recognition of the purpose.

D.H.: *What do you feel are some of the greatest challenges facing the members of the Church of Religious Science in terms of work, livelihood and life purpose?*

R.G.: I think the greatest challenges facing our members are uncertainty and insecurity. Things are changing so quickly they don't know where it's going. Traditional work structures are collapsing; downsizings, rightsizings, retirement plans, permanence, benefits—all of this is changing so fast.

Especially for the younger people, it must be so difficult coming into this workplace with the expectations their families gave them. The rules [are] changing so quickly, and the new rules are less than "visible."

Uncertainty. I think this is one of the reasons that people are drawn to Religious Science, [to] spirituality and religion in general. Once again, we are seeking some certainty in life, some definition: What's it all about?

D.H.: *Yours as well as many new "mega" churches are growing rapidly. What are these churches' roles in terms of community?*

R.G.: They give some sense of connectedness, a way to communicate with someone else, a forum to understand why all of this is going on. We offer a place to deal with uncertainty. I think community and the Internet is a great example of how interconnectedness is growing at an astonishing rate. Community comes from people seeking connectedness. This has been going on for a long time. If we are open to the changes in technology, we can see it is happening in powerful new ways.

D.H.: *Do you believe people have a unique purpose?*

R.G.: We are each a unique expression of a greater thing called God, but we are a unique expression *through our choices*. We are not a unique expression through predestination, predetermination. I believe God has an infinite basket of designs. We access those designs through our mind and the choices we make. It is through our initiative absolutely. Otherwise, we are just sucked into race consciousness, cultural issues, some mass design.

D.H.: *So you're saying we can choose full potential, we can choose to become unique, or we can choose to become a part of this mass of humanity?*

R.G.: Which is still unique within itself. Because we cannot *not* choose. We always choose.

D.H.: *Sharon Bray was pretty courageous with us. When I asked about her success models for clients, she responded that the key was the client's initiative. Without that, the best services in the world had little value.*

R.G.: To me, this is why we are talking about risk. Initiative embraces risk. It holds our purpose. It is absolutely key. She said that? Fascinating.

D.H.: *There is a significant difference between creative thinking and creativity. Often, people who would describe themselves as spiritually driven have a contempt for the commercial and the earthly. They may be smiling, but the contempt bars them from getting results. What do you have to say about that?*

R.G.: It's about ignoring law, ignoring cause and effect. By doing that, we don't succeed on either side—where we are very creative and yet ineffective in the world or [where] we are making money and not using the full potential of our spiritual awareness.

D.H.: *How would you coach them to integrate the two?*

R.G.: Be willing to do whatever is necessary, no matter how mundane or frightening it is. Don't put yourself above the nitty-gritty part of making something happen. Be realistic about what's around you and what you need.

D.H.: *If you were coaching a parent to prepare a child for the workplace, what would you tell them?*

R.G.: Take nothing for granted. Know that change is in the core of being a parent.

D.H.: *What would you like the readers of* The Truth About Work *to hear about work?*

R.G.: Work is good. It is fulfilling. There is no work that is more or less than other work—as long as you feel you are fulfilling a purpose and serving yourself, those around you, that you are serving the higher good.

D.H.: *What do you want to leave behind?*

R.G.: Nothing. As long as I'm doing and working, intuitively, within the context of higher purpose, I have absolutely no thoughts on what I'm going to leave behind.

"I have absolutely no thoughts on what I'm going to leave behind." Can you see the level of living in the moment that takes? To be so fully present to the work at hand that we don't think about the future?

Let's visit someone else. In Los Angeles, there is a church called the Agape Center of Truth. In nine years, Agape has grown to over 5,000 members, with over 12,000 participating friends and over 20 ministries whose work ranges from children's education to feeding the homeless. One of my dear friends said that when she first visited Agape, she realized that God really existed. The Agape Center of Truth has rapidly grown into one of the largest multicultural churches in the United States. Walking into a service at Agape is like walking into the United Nations.

At the center of this organization is Michael Beckwith. Michael comes from an unbounded enthusiasm for living a spiritual life. His energy transcends quotations and dogma. I brought our colleague, Gilda Matthews, a member of Agape as well as a close friend to Michael, on this interview. Gilda had just received her doctorate in psychology and brought a great energy to the meeting.

David Harder: *You have said that God has designed each one of us to have a unique purpose and that until we step into that purpose, we suffer. How does an individual find his or her right purpose?*

Michael Beckwith: First let's define and distinguish purpose. The purpose for all of us is to reveal the love of God. Each of us reveals that purpose in our own unique way. That is why we are here.

The challenge from our particular culture is that we become initiated into materialism, getting and acquiring because we are so afraid of death. Many of us carry a consciousness that life is finite, that on one day, we are born and then on one other day, we are going to die. An individual filled with fear is always trying to get, horde, protect and defend themselves. That is a difficult state of mind for introducing God's unique purpose and unique expression to them.

An individual who is initiated into a spiritual culture carries the gift of the eternal. That gift fosters peace. It fosters patience. What you are doing is very important because in our culture, thoughts of materialism, of fear, of death, of acquisitions pervade the very nature of work in unhealthy ways.

Generally, people come to spiritual teachings when they realize, usually through a crisis or an insight, that life has become meaningless. When they start questioning life at this level, we often find they unleash the dreams that have been hidden for some time, the very dreams they talked about as a child.

As children, our conversations hinted to our possibilities. These possibilities may not be specific like "I'm going to be a fireman," but there are hints of the talents, the feelings, the tonalities. If we listen closely, the purpose is in there.

D.H.: *There is a common theme that when people embrace a spiritual life, the work they have been doing progressively becomes more painful.*

M.B.: If they're doing the wrong thing, absolutely.

D.H.: *When someone comes to you and asks you how to move beyond that work, what do you tell them?*

M.B.: Do what's fun. Basically, find something that makes you laugh, that you love, that you get lost in. People who are in their right path? You can't tell if they are playing or working.

In our culture, it is difficult to accept that, because of the

Protestant work ethic, which tells us we should suffer to work. If it isn't difficult, it doesn't have value. That's not true. It is not in keeping with the way the universe works, the way things really are. When we are in accord, we don't apply effort; we release the gift. When we do that, our finances, our relationships, all that is part of the gestalt is handled.

People are afraid of that. Your internal structures have to be very strong to carry happiness. It takes a degree of inner strength to just be happy. We set up tremendous ceilings and roadblocks to keep happiness.

D.H.: *Describe your work?*

M.B.: I love what I do. What I have to watch is periodically taking downtime. But most of the time, I love what I do.

As I look at the dreams I had as a child, I had three hints of my possibility. I wanted to heal cancer, I wanted to write music and I wanted to lead a spiritual life.

I so much didn't like the idea of being a minister that I stayed away from it as long as I could. I wanted to be in the closet with my spiritual practice, doing meditation and prayer. The rest of the time, I wanted to be out in the world. As I continued my practice, it became apparent that my life and work were going to be the same, which is about meditation and prayer.

It eventually all fit, but I had to break through my own personality. I'm a shy person. I had to become more public, and that required that I grow beyond myself.

D.H.: *What did you bring to this community that prompted it to grow so quickly and become so strong?*

M.B.: Vision. I don't think anything is impossible. I know that spirit is not bound by precedent. So I'm not concerned in how it is going to happen. I'll go for it.

I'm considered a rule breaker. We have so many ministers, in all walks of life, that have gone through their particular schools. They've read about Jesus. When they get up to speak, they are quoting from other people. It's theory. I can tell in 30 to 40 seconds of listening if that person really knows God. Yes, we have to have an intellectual grasp as a platform, but if we don't eventually let go and leap, we don't have anything!

Gilda Matthews: *Could you tell us more about your vision? You told us, based on what you had seen in other ministers, that you didn't want to become a minister. How did you reach this vision?*

M.B.: In opening myself up to my life's work. It had something to do with this tonal quality. I wanted to feel spontaneous. I didn't want to have to work for that feeling. Prior to this work, I was in politics, which was quite toxic, [and] where I had to fit into other people's formats, where they dictated my behavior. I wanted this feeling of spontaneity with my work. So today, I may say, "Four more bars!" I do what I feel like doing. Oh, the services have a certain start time and end time, but within that, I've given myself the freedom to do anything I want for fellowship, for community and for love.

D.H.: *Michael, many of our readers are not living in spiritual communities. Many of them are reading* The Truth About Work *because their lives are "at risk." They may be deeply frightened because of the changes in the world around them. What do you want them to hear?*

M.B.: Basically, the circumstances are not what's important. It is the thoughts we have about it that determine the outcome. If we are on an adventure, the outcome is completely different than if we are coming from expecting the worst.

If I said to the two of you, "This morning, let's have an adventure. Let's get in the car and drive up the coast. I don't know how much money you have in your pocket. I don't even know how much money I have. We just go. We just want to see what happens. We're all in the spirit of adventure, and we are in agreement we are going to have a good time. We will create an experience. We will have exactly the amount of money we need.

We will have the exact amount of gas that we need. We'll run into the right people to run into in order to have a good time, the consciousness of adventure will create an experience, and we will come back and say, "Guess what happened? We went up to Malibu, and we met this guy. And we didn't have enough money to eat out, but these people invited us into their house, and we had a wonderful time."

But if we go out and say, "You know what? I don't have enough money. I don't have much time to play," then we are going to have a completely different experience. We may be depressed. We may be so terrified that we don't do anything. We may say, "Never mind, let's just stay in this room today." We lock the doors and make sure bad things don't happen to us.

If someone is in terror, we have somehow to let them know that how they are looking at a particular situation is going to determine their response to it. But people who are losing jobs may not be in the experience of an adventure; they may be locked in the consciousness of survival. People who are in survival consciousness are fueled by fear.

D.H.: *Here's a dilemma: As we eliminate rote work, low-income workers are being sent back to poverty-stricken neighborhoods without jobs. Perhaps even more important, they've been sent back without answers. They have inadequate information on how to dig themselves out of it. Unless we take a collective responsibility, we are all at risk.*

M.B.: I agree. When we look at the lowest rungs of society, that is our measurement of whether we are really a civilized society.

As you said earlier, we are at a turning point, and these factories are now closing. As we shift our priorities in this society, we say people can go to work and reclaim the very areas of society that we have thrown away. Recycling. We have a tremendous amount of work to do in this area. We've polluted rivers, lakes, oceans; our major cities are filled with litter; we have metals stuck in junkyards that are just sitting there, decaying. This is an analogy of our people, just sitting there as unrealized potential.

As a culture, we are having a new adventure. If we simply say, "Business as usual," we are talking about a level of destruction that we create in our reality, such as producing more have-nots, breeding another level of poverty, crime and despair.

Or we can begin to galvanize a new vision. It doesn't have to happen within the government. It happens by individuals networking just like we are.

How are we going to change this culture? I don't know. But I do know that if I have an adventurous spirit and know it is possible, the idea will come because it is in our consciousness.

D.H.: *What is your truth about work?*

M.B.: I pay attention to Kahlil Gibran's quote: "Work is love made visible."

In the old Protestant work ethic, we simply measured productivity; beauty was something extra. Joyful work has to have a component of beauty. It is spontaneous. Nothing stays the same. Things are always getting better because a life of beauty produces a life of excellence.

As much as we might try to separate our work life from our personal life, the two are inextricably linked. In order to live a balanced life, it is important to maintain the same moral and ethical standards at work as you do at home.

When asked about the nature and meaning of work, Marianne Williamson, the author of *A Return to Love, A Woman's Worth* and *Illuminata*, shared this with us:

For many Americans, most of our day is spent at work. We often spend more time with our coworkers than with our families. The relationships we have in that arena directly impact the fabric of our emotional lives. You can't keep your heart closed or your integrity and excellence on hold in that area and expect the rest of life to feel good.

The issues I see most magnified in the work setting are those having to do with balancing kindness and compassion with healthy boundaries and high work standards. All those things are necessary to right living, and integrating them within ourselves is the work of today's new-paradigm frontiersmen.

We are entering the workplace of truth. What does that mean? Think of the dialogues from everyone who contributed. Think of the changes we have discussed. All that matters is truth. For years, especially in industrialized America, we simply felt we couldn't tell the truth and get away with it. Now it is imperative. When we introduce truth into the workplace, spirituality naturally emerges. For when we tell the truth about what is occurring, when we tell the truth about our needs and culture, and when we tell the truth about work, all solutions are spiritual. No longer do we find our solutions in the external world; we find them through our ultimate truth—that all is God.

For Reflection

1. How would you describe the health of your spirit, or, if you care to describe it as such, your spirituality in your work?

2. What were your reactions to Bob's, Michael's and Marianne's input?

3. How could you strengthen spirituality in your work?

4. How can you actively support workplace spirituality in your colleagues?

11

The Workplace of Truth

I NEVER DID A DAY'S WORK IN

MY LIFE. IT WAS ALL FUN.

—THOMAS A. EDISON

The new workplace represents an opportunity, a possibility, a turning point and a choice: heaven or hell, have or have not. We move toward hell by clinging to a world that has vanished. We move into heaven by surrendering to change and, while doing so, staying focused on spirit. A free fall, if you will. It is in that free fall that we realize spirit never abandons us. Free will has given us the ability to abandon spirit, which continues in spite of our distraction. Unfortunately, the distraction draws us into the machine where, as Gandhi said, "We work but no longer live."

The new workplace is an opportunity given to us by vast changes and redefinitions. It is a workplace of spiritual expression and unique gifts, a workplace that rewards us for our point of view. In this new workplace, most of us no longer deliver rote and monotonous work. We don't even have to work in cubicles unless it makes sense. We no longer climb corporate ladders as a reward for being a "better machine."

Some of us don't feel prepared for this new world. We are frightened by the light, at the prospect of full living. As Marianne Williamson once said, "It is our power, not our weakness, that most frightens us."

Spiritual evolution isn't putting on the brakes out of sympathy for our weakness. We are being asked to stand up. To deliver. To participate in a new workplace that doesn't reward us for passivity. In the new workplace, we can no longer afford to think about the life we might have lived. We must live in order to do the work of value. Remember, the work of value is usually an act of joy. In the new workplace, the only communication that matters is the truth. In fact, the truth is our most important asset.

I don't wish to trivialize our dialogue by giving a few snap outcomes and predictions. I do know we have profound changes in front of us, each one accompanied by a choice. Following are just a few.

Life Purpose vs. Job Description

As we've discussed, a fixed job description isn't fluid enough to respond to the chaos and rate of change occurring in business. Job descriptions are no longer the most efficient means of delivering work. The only way we can succeed in a world where information and change arrive at the speed of light is to go within and define ourselves from that place. That is a revolutionary shift for us, but it is a change that brings an opportunity for real joy in our work.

What we are doing becomes obsolete in a moment. Therefore, our awareness of greater purpose becomes ever more critical. That purpose exists in our truth. The truth already exists. In this new world, each and every one of us must tell the truth of what we were designed to do. If it takes meditation, if it takes conversation, if it requires going to the mat—regardless of how we get it, whatever it takes, remember: The truth is a requirement for survival in this new world. It is also a cornerstone of happiness.

Without that truth, we are simply swept away by change. Torrents of information rage past us and overcome those of us who insist on clinging to the aimlessness of the industrial and media-distraction worlds.

What is your truth? In the new workplace, we can no longer afford to shrug our shoulders. Succeeding in this new world requires that each of us actively pursue the identification of truth. No other information is relevant.

In chaos, each one of us must visit our center and stay defined in our truth. The reward? We stop suffering. Breaking from the cultural restrictions imposed on us and stepping into our unique life purpose ends a life without purpose. We become aware of why we are here. We simply allow the truth of why we are here to emerge. As we package it, we charge money for it!

Spirit-driven life purpose ends our empty worship of organizational hierarchy, machinelike job descriptions and hostile takeovers. They become meaningless gestures of the chaos.

The good news: We are finally stepping into an era that requires us to do what we love. This is a time when we can break from the culture that treated work simply as a source of survival. We now have an imperative to treat our work as our life. As we make that definition, we not only upgrade our ability to succeed in the world; we step into our spiritual possibility. Only from that place can we find the integration of spirit and economic needs.

The bad news: Increased change and chaos will destroy anyone embracing aimlessness. The "have-nots" could wage unprecedented war. Some of us don't have enough access to information to even hear this message. Unless those of us who hear it carry the message forward, collectively, we're in trouble.

Communication vs. Commuting

It costs far more to give you a cubicle to work in than a cellular phone and a modem. The revolution in where we work is just beginning. Communications technology is prompting us to question the sanity of herding thousands of people into buildings when we can deliver our work anywhere and at any time. These changes don't eliminate every commute but they do introduce a new series of possibilities, as far as the optimum way to package your work:

Telecommuting from home

Working out of your car

Working from the woods

Working in a mini office that is only two miles from your home, rather than 30 miles away

The good news: An opportunity to satisfy lifestyle requirements as well as work needs. For those of us who want to work at home, we can do that more effectively than ever. For those of us who want to live in a particular place, we now have the communications mobility to do it.

The bad news:

What new challenges do we face by isolating workers from each other?

How do we stay connected?

What will happen if our primary connectedness is a computer screen?

There are predictions our office high-rises will become empty monoliths. Personally, I don't buy this. But who knows?

Business Needs vs. Jobs for Life

Let's put on our sanity hats for a moment.

If today's business needs change and transform on a daily basis, why would we create a job for life to fulfill a temporal need? How could such a job continue to be satisfying? (Other than in a coma.)

The new workplace is no longer beholden to jobs. It is beholden to the work at hand. It is served by workers who fluidly respond to immediate needs, not goal programs. The successful workers package their unique purpose and deliver it to the place that needs the value. Then, they move on.

In this new world, the following truth is required:

What is my purpose?
Where am I most needed?
When is my work complete?
Is it time to move on?

The good news: We have never been given a landscape filled with more opportunity for the creative and adaptive worker.

The bad news: For those of us who believe we are not creative and adaptive, remember the phrase "pushed by the pain until we are pulled by the vision"? It is time to redefine the very nature of our life. Get mentors, coaches, education and help.

Collaborative Effort vs. Hierarchy

In a world where business moves at the speed of light, hierarchy has very little value. In fact, it usually gets in the way of business. We have a new workplace where people collaborate constantly. This is great news! No longer able to work in covertness, which was biologically harmful, we now work together in identifying, promoting, upholding and working with . . . the truth!

Collaboration, as Jack Canfield stated, is needed to do something huge. Collaboration is needed to produce comfort, education, mentoring, coaching and support systems.

The good news: It is only healthy.

The bad news: There are still a number of aging middle managers, scared stiff, in their offices. Go find them and show them how to live in the new milieu.

Work for Life vs. Imposed Retirement

When we establish a life purpose, no one can impose the end of our work. We work as long as it brings us joy and brings value to the world.

The good news: Many of us will stop dropping dead within a year after having our work and our purpose severed. We will continue to be vital and healthy and contributive.

The bad news: Some of us have been retired from the day we started to work.

Entrepreneurism vs. Paternal Employment

The day of the job for life within the multinational company is over. This doesn't mean the day of the multinational company is over. It means that even if we take a job in such a company, the nature of work and business has become so fluid that we must treat our work as an entrepreneurial activity. No longer clocking in and clocking out. No longer assuming that if we just focus on rote and monotonous routines, our income is handled. If you have any doubts about this, revisit Sharon Bray's conversation with us about AT&T.

Being clear on our purpose; marketing and selling our purpose; watching the market for changes that we can use; building effective support systems for our success; defining on a daily basis our happiness and our needs—all of these characteristics are embraced by the successful entrepreneur. Now, in this new world, they are embraced by the successful worker.

The good news: We have an opportunity to make more money by producing more value if we embrace the ground rules. We are facing a business landscape that gives us much more vitality and excitement, more than we could have imagined in the old world.

The bad news: Some of us didn't want to be that excited or that awake.

Balance vs. the "Rodent Wheel"

If more is being expected of us—if, in truth, we are being asked to "wake up"—then it is only natural that we want more balance in our lives. In a world of value, we want healthy personal lives and family lives. We want physical health and a fulfilling romantic life. In this new world, the expectation of fulfillment and satisfaction is taking precedence over the insane notion that it is worth it to continue working that hard with that little payoff when we get home. This is also an outcome of spiritual evolution. There is more to life than making a buck. There is also more to spirit than monastic living.

The good news: Many of us are already achieving this. Once we take a stand for it, it can happen more quickly than we think.

The bad news: Some of us still don't believe it is possible.

Spiritual Fulfillment vs. Being a Machine

Do what you love. Remember Michael Beckwith's comment: "People who are in their right path? You can't tell if they are playing or working."

The good news: This is the truth. This is where we are headed.

The bad news: All those who refuse truth will get their noses rubbed in untruth. No one deserves that.

If you don't believe it, turn to page 1 and start over. Discuss *The Truth* with a friend. Call us. Challenge us. We're up to it.

Get into the community and find the spirit that exists in everyone.

Live purpose. Live well.

Epilogue

Where did I come from? Who wrote this book? The more I do this work, the more I realize it is more challenging to tell you who I am, rather than offering up a biography or résumé. So I'm going to weave the truth into what we usually do, which is offer up a biography or a résumé.

I grew up in a little town called Beaumont, California—essentially 6,000 people waiting to die near the edge of the desert. If that sounds deeply cynical, then why does a town of 6,000 have nine rest homes? Anyway, if you want to see it, look for the concrete dinosaurs as you drive out to Palm Springs.

I was adopted by a fairly well-to-do couple, an immigrant physician and his wife, both Seventh-Day Adventists. I was taught at an early age to fear them and especially, to fear God. In *The Truth About Work,* I'm not drawn to go into any detail about the suffering that existed in my family and the house I grew up in. What I do choose to convey is that love and making ourselves available to spirit heals anything.

I am a living and breathing testimony to the power of love, spirituality, therapy and good clothes. When I was five, they discovered I had a powerful talent for music. Music was my ticket out of there. It became my protective shield for much of my life. I created protection by being the best at whatever I did and by striking awe into the people that heard me. Unfortunately, that dance didn't save me from myself. When I was 18, I was accepted into a piano performance program at USC, where I excelled and envisioned a life as a concert pianist. By the time I hit my mid-20s, I was a confirmed alcoholic, playing "I Shot the Sheriff" in a road band where everyone's outfit matched.

My family had taught me that "money fixes everything." So, at 24, I cut my hair, got sober and within two years, was the youngest area manager in a multinational placement company. I spent the next 13 years working in the employment industry, displaying every accoutrement of financial success. My 12-Step program had given me a dictate: If I was to stay sober, I had to find a power greater than myself. Thus far, the only power greater than myself had been my dad, who beat me, and an angry, white, male God who was waiting to beat me when I died.

My commitment to recovery was so deep that I was willing to do anything. So I studied; I worked with spiritual masters; I took up meditation; I participated in virtually any seminar or workshop that appeared to have value; I went into intensive therapy; and I learned how to pray.

In my mid-30s, I was still working in the placement field. I was making great money, but where was the value? Outside of making money, I didn't see much purpose to what I was doing. Ironically, I was also growing as a musician, recording and working with some of the best performers in the industry, headlining at great clubs. I have found that many of us get trapped in our own ideas of what we are "supposed" to do. I am a very talented musician, and I have given my gift a great deal of energy. At that time, I was also trapped by my gift. Here was an even greater possibility sitting in the wings, but because music was a lifelong quest, that was what I was "supposed" to do. It was all planned: I would leave the employment industry, fueled by a lucrative recording contract. I would make great money as a musician, and that would be the end of it.

At that time, I was working with a powerful producer, who became a dear friend. Then, at 38, he dropped dead of a heart attack. It all hit me: I was living my life as if it were a dress rehearsal. Everything would turn out when I got this contract, this car, this vacation, this outcome. Very much like Michael Beckwith discussed: Happiness was "out there," in the future. I remember sitting on the beach in front of my home in Malibu. I had worked so hard to get this home. I sat on the beach twice in a year. I was so busy working to pay for this lifestyle that I rarely had time to enjoy it. And my work? I was getting ready for, driving to, being at, driving home from and recovering from something that I, in truth, loathed.

It all started out on a fairly maudlin level. I remember getting on my knees and praying—no, snorting—"What will you have me do, Lord?" I knew in my heart that if I had survived my life, if I had recovered as much as I had and if I was going to really live, there had to be a greater possibility for me. There had to be a life that I didn't need to recover from.

In the beginning of my search, I went to an academic career counselor, and after poking holes in paper all day, I was told I had a personality type that could make a good research librarian or civil engineer. I responded, "Ten minutes of that, and I'll be hanging dead from the ceiling."

I was sitting in a human potential program, and it all dawned on me. The participants were standing up and making grandiose declarations of what they were going to do when they left the program. It dawned on me that what I viewed as common sense was actually a deep and powerful natural gift. I realized I had the ability to guide people to conclusions about their work by asking the right questions. What would happen if I refined the skill? It also started to hit me that I would be able to make peace with my life if I made peace with the portions of my life that I held up as "detours."

In our culture, we set up so many boxes. We box ourselves in because we are afraid of our own power. I sought comfort from my unhappiness in my ego. As a "genius" musician, the employment industry had been a miserable, even surreal detour. But when I connected with spirit, I started to get the difference between ego and spirit. Spirit brought value to all of my waking moments. If God had been with me all the time, then everything I had experienced had value.

The quickest and most efficient career development

program is prayer. We don't have to be perfect to pray. In God's eyes, we already are perfect. We don't have to have a weak ego to pray. In God's eyes, our ego isn't kid stuff. In recognizing that God was with me all the time, regardless of what I was experiencing, and that all that drove my life came from love, who was I to keep snivelin'? Why would I possibly stand in the way of what I was designed to do, when in prayer, I realized I didn't have a better idea?

I became a work expert because I was miserable in my work. I help people with their careers because I haven't found anyone who was more miserable in their work than I. In growing up, I get to demonstrate my biggest leap, and that doesn't happen when I play small. In recognizing that all of my waking moments were valuable— all my efforts, missteps and insights, every painful circumstance and joyful breakthrough—I got my life. I realized that every moment was valuable when I realized that God was there.

I was led into this work. After 13 years in the employment industry, it was clear to me that all the spiritual growth in the world wouldn't produce a paycheck if it wasn't married to a business proposition. It was also clear that our culture was in need of a tool kit for accessing the *spiritual intention* of our work.

Where did this come from? I can only say it came from my spirit after I started sincerely asking, "Why am I here?" I had always wanted to impact people. I had always wanted to make my life an act of love. The means kept eluding me because I kept avoiding a full measure of spirit.

I was virtually guided to design Careermotion's first

seminar. Seven years ago, we delivered the program at the Loew's Beach Hotel in Santa Monica. We had 36 professionals in the room—attorneys, psychologists, entrepreneurs, the young, the old, the rich, the stuck. Two nights later, I sat in my car and wept. We had 36 miracles. Each person in that room had experienced a profound upleveling in his or her relationship to work. Each person walked out of there with an awareness of what he or she was designed to do and how to do that in a healthy way.

All of that came from a place I can't explain, a place where no one can tell me how to do it. This work has given effortless meaning to my life. I choose to use the word *effortless* because for so many years, I was applying great effort to finding meaning in my life. Now, my life is quite simply about miracles. For me, it doesn't get any better than that. Now, I know that our lives are an act of love. When we step into our authentic, God-given life purpose, everything that is false, everything that is untrue, slips away. Today, to sit in the presence of business, spiritual and artistic leaders discussing the power and glory of the human spirit that shows up in work— this is my miracle. In delivering this work, I get to experience a level of creativity and performance that my years of music and artistic work prepared me for. In stepping into my spiritual intention of work, I get to experience creativity and performance that go beyond my best musical performances.

All of us have that possibility. Everyone has the design that no one else has. Step into it. I know that if such a wonderful life can come out of the life I had, anything— absolutely anything—is possible.

Appendix

Old World vs. New World Workplace

Old World Values/Words	New World Values/Words
Competition	Collaboration
Job Description	Unique Gift
Hierarchy	Flat Organization
Survival	Passion
Jobs for Life	Entrepreneurism
Machinelike	Creative
Organizational Agenda	Organizational Spirit
Quantity	Value
Industrial Age	Knowledge Age
Job	Life Purpose
Predictability	Daily Change
Jobs	Project Work
Standardized Life	Unique Life Purpose
Creative Thinking	Creativity
Mission Statements	Mission Questions
Monastic Spirituality	Community Spirit
Covertness	Truth

The Path of Life Purpose: Its Obstacles

Choice	("I don't know.")
Declare it	("You're crazy.")
Draw attention to yourself	("They'll hurt me.")
Build effective support systems	("What's that?")
Success	("No obstacle.")

Glossary

comfort. Used to shut down the fear mechanism.

comfort tribe. A group of people committed to our well-being.

culture of distraction. A culture rich with opportunities to avoid risk, life, life purpose and truth. Includes television, the Internet, computer games, in-line skating, movies, gyms—all good if not used for the purpose of avoiding life possibility.

entrepreneurism. In the new work world, entrepreneurism reflects more than starting a business; it signifies a state of mind. The entrepreneurism of the employed worker is mainly a reflection of the work components an effective entrepreneur embraces. These include a business plan, a marketing plan, daily sales activity, strong business management and a solid support network. In today's business climate, these are components that will be built into any employee's work strategy. It doesn't mean employees are "entrepreneurs"; it means they have learned from the entrepreneur.

Small-business owners are not true entrepreneurs. They have a business that has produced a job for themselves. True entrepreneurs create jobs for others. They usually want to change the world. They think big, they play big. Entrepreneurs are the individuals fueling the growth in the new work world.

flat organization. A contemporary organizational structure without middle managers and extensive hierarchy.

haves (new version). Creative and adaptive individuals armed with the awareness of their purpose and the awareness of how to succeed in that purpose.

have-nots (new version). Individuals who not only are "underemployed," but who don't have adequate information for surviving in the new work world.

information filters. These are the attitudes or beliefs that determine how we react to information that is confrontational, frightening and that prompts us to grow. We use these filters to kill off opportunity. Hence, we kill off portions of our lives. The four information filters are: aimlessness, contempt, cynicism and resignation.

job description. A description of one's tasks and one's turf.

life purpose. Much more than a job description, it is the meaning we give to our lives; it is what we have to contribute. Life purpose encompasses our unique gift and personal commitment. It often includes a description of a difference we want to make in the world.

passion. An intense enthusiasm that overcomes obstacles, challenges and problems. The fuel of the value-driven worker.

predictability. The core promise to the worker during the industrial revolution: "Work in this world, and we will give predictable employment and outcomes."

rodent wheel. Too busy, too tired, too dissatisfied to be available for an effective and happy life.

snivelin'. The alternative to full living and full healing.

substandards. Any standards that drain the life out of our lives.

survival. The primary standard applied to work during the industrial revolution. This standard means we settle for paying for our lifestyle. It is based on productivity rather than beauty. It is an outcome of the old Protestant work ethic.

telecommuting. Signifies that work is done via telecommunications channels, which frees individuals from being dependent on driving to work. Uses faxes, e-mail, modems, Internet, satellite, laptop computers, electronic conferencing, etc.

tribe. A group of people with shared values, rituals, rites of passage and costumes.

uplevel. The process of raising our standards and consequently taking the action necessary to realize real-world results.

value. Adds something of importance to the world or the individual's life. After careful "evaluation," justifies the expenditure of money or time.

Bibliography

Boldt, Laurence G. *Zen and the Art of Making a Living.* New York: Penguin Books, 1993.

Bridges, William. *JobShift.* Reading, Mass.: Addison-Wesley, 1994.

Camp, Wesley D. *What a Piece of Work Is Man!* New York: Prentice-Hall, 1990.

Carnegie, Dale. *Dale Carnegie's Scrapbook.* New York: Simon & Schuster, 1959.

John-Roger and Peter McWilliams. *The Portable Life 101.* Los Angeles: Prelude Press, 1992.

For More Information

How can you bring the concepts from *The Truth About Work* into your organization? Careermotion Programs are delivered in multiple markets throughout the world and include:

The Truth About Work Program (Individuals)

"Define your dreams and make them come true." A two-day seminar that prompts workers to define upgrades in every area of their work lives. This is the environment that initiated *The Truth About Work*.

The Truth About Teams (Organizations)

A revolutionary Socratic process that builds authentic teams, yet pulls workers away from their stations for a few hours. Potent and economical.

The Truth About Success (Organizations)

Takes troubled workers and prompts them to design their own healthy solution to the problem in a few days.

The Truth About Sales (Organizations/Individuals)
Get over the fear of selling and learn to win business by asking the right questions versus making a "pitch." A one-day training.

Licensing
Careermotion welcomes new colleagues. All programs are available for license to qualified facilitators. Call for details.

For more information contact:
Careermotion,™ Inc.
2040 Avenue of the Stars
Ste. 400
Los Angeles, CA 90067
(888) U BE-TRUE